Kate

THE
KATHARINE HEPBURN
ALBUM

Lauren Tarshis

A PERIGEE BOOK

Perigee Books
are published by
The Putnam Publishing Group
200 Madison Avenue
New York, NY 10016

Library of Congress Cataloging-in-Publication Data

Tarshis, Lauren.
    Kate : the Katharine Hepburn album / Lauren Tarshis.
        p.   cm.
    ISBN 0-399-51790-1
    1. Hepburn, Katharine, 1909–   .   2. Motion picture actors
and actresses—United States—Biography.   I. Title.
    PN2287.H45T37   1993
    791.43′028′092—dc20   92-34140 CIP
    [B]

Cover design by Isabella Fasciano
Cover photo © by Ben Carbonetto
Printed in the United States of America
1   2   3   4   5   6   7   8   9   10

This book is printed on acid-free paper.

∞

To Nettie Tarshis

(MOMA)

Acknowledgments

Special thanks to Chaya Deisch, for her tremendous research help; Patty Brown and John Boswell; Ron and Howard Mandelbaum of Photofest; Ben Carbonetto of The Kobal Collection; and Mary Corliss of the Museum of Modern Art. I would also like to thank David, Leo, my parents, Andrew, Dee, Cathy and Michele, for their great support and love.

Contents

Introduction:
A Timeless Woman

A number of years ago, Katharine Hepburn was swimming laps when she noticed a young girl perched at the top of a diving tower that stood about twelve feet high. Several times the girl crept close to the edge, trying to muster up the courage to jump. But as Kate said, "She could never quite dare to do it."

So Kate decided to climb up the tower, plastic hip and all, and make the dive herself. "I did that just for you," she told the little girl after emerging from the pool. "The only thing you have to do is make up your mind to do it. When you get up there, don't stop. Don't look down, just do it."

Few episodes in Kate's life so neatly sum up her essence—the power that has fueled one of Hollywood's greatest careers. At eighty-five years old, she is still very much the same woman she was when she first arrived in Hollywood in 1931. She has always been bold, independent and, as she would put it, "without much bunk." Never in her life has she shied away from a high dive.

Her potent spirit didn't always go over well in Hollywood, and at times it appeared as though she would be banished for good. But she always survived, saved by her own inner strength and the respect of

Kate during her first months in Hollywood. (MOMA)

important people—moguls, producers, directors and others—who valued this woman of substance in a business based on ego and not much else.

Today, Katharine Hepburn is admired as much (or perhaps more) than she was at the height of her Hollywood glamour days in the thirties and forties. Her older fans have stood by her for nearly seven decades, through countless ebbs and flows in her movie career. And a new generation of young fans, turned on to Kate by late-night and Sunday afternoon television, consistently rate her among the Americans they most admire.

How has she endured? Certainly not by courting her fans. Anyone who's ever asked for an autograph or tried to sneak a peek at her Connecticut retreat knows that she does not relish personal contact with her admirers. One autograph-seeker, rebuffed by Kate, told her that she should be more polite. "After all," the fan said, "we made you what you are today." Kate responded without a pause, "Like hell you did."

She's a product of her background, of parents "who did things that mattered" and pushed her to know her limits only so that she could constantly exceed them. She was and still is a beauty. But she was never a screen goddess; her charms were always of the more earthly variety—a mixture of New England salt and grit within a body with more sharp edges than curves.

She endures because she never doubted that she would, and who were we to disagree? As her friend Garson Kanin once wrote: "In the largest sense, Katharine Hepburn's popularity has never waned because people know (magically, intuitively) that she stands for something, even if many of them have no clear idea as to what that something is. They recognize that in a time of dangerous conformity, and the fear of being different, here is one who stands up gallantly to the killing wave."

Kate

"I'm really just a shadow of them."

THROUGHOUT HER SIXTY-YEAR CAREER, Katharine Hepburn has been asked to account for her extraordinary success. Certainly talent has something to do with it, as does luck, timing and whatever hidden forces guide some people into their dreams and others in the opposite direction.

But looking back on her life, Kate has repeatedly ceded all credit for her success and happiness to her parents—"fascinating people" whose passion and boldness have inspired Kate throughout her life. "I'm really just a shadow of them," she says.

Kate was born on May 12, 1907, in Hartford, Connecticut. She was the second of six children born to a couple whose lives were indeed as dramatic as any film their daughter starred in.

Kate's mother, born Katharine Marta Houghton, was a Boston blue blood. She had a striking face and a great figure set off by a nineteen-inch waist. She also had a family fortune behind her. Her grandfather was the founder of Corning Glass.

"Kit" Houghton enjoyed the opportunities that came with money

A Hepburn family portrait, minus Dr. Hepburn, circa 1914. (BEN CARBONETTO)

and privilege. But the life she crafted for herself defied many of the customs of her class. It was a life driven by her brains and principles, not unlike the life led by the daughter she would name after herself.

Kit was orphaned when she was sixteen. Her father, whose personal business failures had estranged him from his family, committed suicide with a bullet to the head. Four months later, her mother, whom Kit adored, was diagnosed with stomach cancer. Within four months, she was dead. And Kit and her two younger sisters were sent to Corning, New York, to live with their father's brother, Amory Houghton, the head of the thriving Corning Glass empire.

Uncle Amory was a businessman who took his role of guardian seriously. And he had clear plans for his three nieces. He would send them to finishing school if they wished. Then he would help them marry into appropriate families.

Kit, however, had other plans. Her mother had always insisted that her daughters would go to college. She even had one in mind, Bryn Mawr, a prestigious women's college outside of Philadelphia. Kit and her sisters were determined to make good on their mother's wish, which she reiterated shortly before she died. But there were obstacles. Like most Americans at the time, Amory Houghton believed that higher education for women was a dubious, perhaps even dangerous, idea. There was also the problem of Bryn Mawr's entrance exam, which rivaled Harvard's and Yale's in its comprehensiveness. Kit's years of schooling had prepared her to run a house full of servants and play a passable sonata. But she lacked the firm grasp of the classics, mathematics, history and the other topics covered on Bryn Mawr's exam.

But Kit was determined. So with the single-mindedness that was by this time a core trait (and a major source of friction with Uncle Amory) Kit plotted to get into Bryn Mawr. She hired expensive tutors to help her cram for the entrance exam. She worked through stacks of classic texts, and mastered years' worth of history and math.

Uncle Amory and Kit had never gotten along particularly well. Amory Houghton didn't appreciate Kit's personality (which he described as "wild"), her unladylike interest in politics and her tendency to scoff at his vision of her future. But Kit's diligence impressed him so much that he escorted her to Bryn Mawr and waited while she took her exam. When Kit found out that she passed the test (just barely), Uncle Amory presided over a small celebration and made sure she understood that he fully supported her efforts to become educated.

Four years at Bryn Mawr refined Kit's intellect and reinforced her desire to define herself outside the upper-crust models provided for her. Her suite of rooms on campus (she and all students had maid service) was a sort of salon where Kit and her classmates would debate issues like women's rights, which would become Kit's calling later in her life. Upon leaving Bryn Mawr in 1899, the yearbook staff asked Kit and her classmates about their future aspirations. Kit's blunt response runs alongside her senior picture: "To raise hell with established conventions."

While Kit was getting herself educated, Thomas Norval Hepburn was hunkering down to become a doctor. He was born in Virginia, where his father was a minister and his mother took in boarders to supplement the family income. Her favored tenants were teachers, who tutored her children in exchange for reduced rent. Despite their limited means, the Hepburn name carried some cachet. Those who cared enough to investigate the Hepburn genealogy would find a strong pedigree back in Scotland, where a forefather had been a lover of Mary, Queen of Scots.

Tom and Kit met in Baltimore, where Tom was pursuing his medical degree at Johns Hopkins University. Kit had moved to Baltimore to live with her sister Edith, who was also a Hopkins medical student (Johns Hopkins was the only medical school open to women at the time). Kit figured that Baltimore, with its stock of university and medical students, would be a fine place to meet eligible young men. She spotted Tom Hepburn during a fencing match. "That one's for me," she told Edith.

Kit and Tom married in November 1904. Not surprisingly, Uncle Amory Houghton did not believe that the penniless son of a Virginia minister was a suitable match for his gifted niece. But as usual, Kit didn't give much thought to her Uncle Amory's opinion. She knew she had made the perfect match, and she was right. Kit and Tom's marriage would last for nearly fifty years, until Kit's death in 1951. For all of their children, including Kate, the bond between Kit and Thomas represented a standard of both love and friendship that would inspire them throughout their lives. "They were a good team," Kate said. "They were very lucky."

The Hepburns settled in Hartford, where Tom had been offered an internship at Hartford Hospital. His interest was urology—an un-

Kate at age three. (MOMA)

common route for a promising young doctor, and not a topic that many turn-of-the-century New Englanders discussed openly. But Thomas saw the chance to contribute to a fast-growing sector of medicine. And like his wife, he didn't care much about the opinions of polite society.

Both Tom and Kit wanted a large family. And within a year of marriage, Kit gave birth to Thomas Norval Hepburn, Jr. Kate followed two years later, named after Kit. By 1915, the brood included six children: Tom, Kate, Richard, Robert, Marion and Margaret. All of the children except for Tom shared the same middle name: Houghton.

The Hepburn parents had definite ideas about child rearing. Dr. Hepburn insisted that each child start the day with a cold shower—his patented method for character building (and a ritual Kate continues to practice). Complaining or "moaning," as Kit called it, was not tolerated. Neither was disrespect toward their parents or bickering among children. Punishments and spankings, as Kate remembers, were doled out liberally. "I was brought up to pay for my own errors," Kate says. "I was spanked pretty often. I think I asked for trouble, and I'm still fairly good at handling it."

But despite a strict code of conduct, the Hepburn house was progressive, even by today's standards. Above all, both Tom, Sr., and Kit wanted their children to be strong and resilient. And whether they were sledding down an icy hill or taking an exam, the children were urged (and sometimes forced) to push their limits. No tree was too tall to climb, no river too cold or rough for swimming and canoeing. "My childhood gave me a freedom from fear," Kate says. "That's what I was trained in. I was riding a bicycle all over Hartford when I was three years old."

Freedom of expression was another rule of the household. Dinner was a free-for-all, an often chaotic session of talk and debate. No topic was taboo, even for the youngest children. Nudism, prostitution, and venereal disease were all ripe topics of conversation at the Hepburn dinner table. "My parents believed that children should never be sent out of the room," Kate says.

Kate and her brothers and sisters grew up watching their parents devote themselves to various causes, often at the expense of their reputations within conservative Hartford society.

Early in his career, Dr. Hepburn used his influence within the medical community to launch a sustained fight against the spread of venereal disease, which was an epidemic before the discovery of antibiotics. Tens of thousands died and scores more were maimed by syphilis and gonorrhea, which were spread chiefly by prostitutes and the men who patronized them. Dr. Hepburn was particularly horrified

(BEN CARBONETTO)

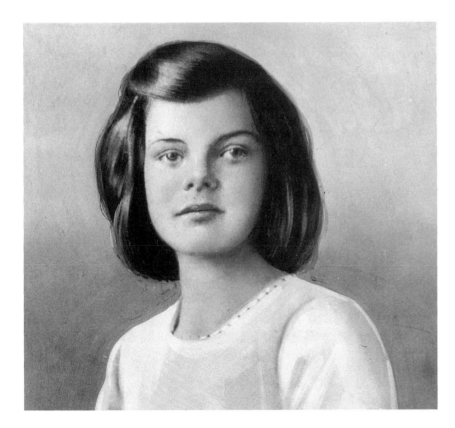

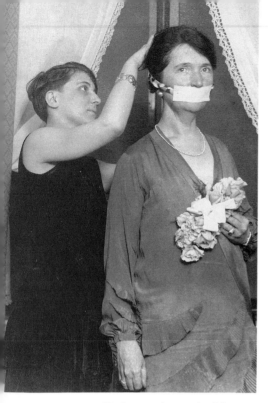

Birth control crusader Margaret Sanger. (BETTMANN ARCHIVE)

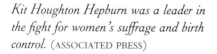

Kit Houghton Hepburn was a leader in the fight for women's suffrage and birth control. (ASSOCIATED PRESS)

by the case of a young mother he treated for advanced gonorrhea. Her husband had visited a brothel on the night before his wedding, and passed the disease on to his wife. She died after several months of suffering.

This case and dozens of others like it prompted Dr. Hepburn to found the Connecticut Social Hygiene Association. It was the least offensive name he could come up with for an organization that would focus on an issue that most people—including many doctors—were too embarrassed or ashamed to talk about. If he lacked drugs that would cure venereal disease (which would remain untreatable until the development of penicillin) he would try to educate the public to curb its spread.

Kit Hepburn joined her husband in his crusade, concentrating her efforts on closing down Hartford's dozens of brothels. But her real interest was women's rights. When Kate was young, Kit was a devoted fighter for women's suffrage. She was a follower of Emmeline Pankhurst, a suffragette leader who also fought for the rights of factory laborers and the urban poor. Like Pankhurst, Kit involved her children in her cause, taking them along to her speaking engagements and protests, where they often marched along with her, placards in hand.

Later, Kit shifted her energies to another women's issue: birth control. She had attended a speech given by Margaret Sanger, whom

she vaguely knew from her years in Corning. Sanger's message was simple: working-class families, she insisted, were often dragged into poverty by their inability to control the number of children they have. Though her six children hardly made her an embodiment of the birth control movement, Kit would embrace this cause for the rest of her life.

Kit became one of Sanger's closest friends, and helped her form the organization that is the legacy of the early birth control movement, Planned Parenthood. "The upper class women all get birth control information from their doctors," Kit said in a 1936 speech. "But the very people who need it most—the people who are poor or on relief—do not."

Kit's involvement in this "radical" movement caused a strain between the Hepburns and many of their conservative neighbors, particularly at Fenwick, the tiny Connecticut beach community where they spent their summers. "We were aware of a lot of opposition when we went to Fenwick," Kate recalls. "Mother was a little bit afraid we'd be snubbed. It was a very conservative place, and they were all Republicans, so they naturally disagreed with everything Mother was fighting for. I knew I wasn't really a member of the club, but I think it affected me very fortunately. It makes you ambitious when you get snubbed a bit. I just thought they were wrong."

Among Kit Hepburn's heroines and fellow crusaders was Emmeline Pankhurst, leader of the women's suffrage movement. (BETTMANN ARCHIVE)

Fenwick, the Hepburn's home on the Connecticut coast, was a "paradise" for Kate and her brothers and sisters. She continues to spend her weekends there. (BETTMANN ARCHIVE)

The Hepburns split their time between Hartford and Fenwick. Unlike Newport, a high-society resort community a bit further up the New England coast, Fenwick was rustic and private, a real retreat. The family's rambling house, situated on a stretch of private beach, was a "paradise" for the family. Dr. Hepburn pushed all his children to be competitive athletes, and Kate particularly excelled. She became an expert in tennis, swimming and golfing. She also discovered a taste for acting. At Fenwick, she was the ringleader of a band of child actors. They spent rainy days in the Hepburn living room, practicing plays to perform for their neighbors. Their most successful production was *Beauty and the Beast*, launched to raise money for children on a Navajo Indian reservation.

Kate still spends most of her weekends and all summers at Fenwick. Even on the coldest mornings of winter, she drags herself down to the water for a quick dip in the Sound—a holdover from the freezing showers of her childhood.

Within the Hepburn clan, Kate was closest to her eldest brother, Tom. Though he was two and a half years older, he was happy to let his scrappy sister tag along with him and his friends. Kate was always much more at home in the sweaty games of her brother and his friends than in the world of dollhouses and tea parties. She recalls intense feelings of jealousy toward her brother because he was a boy. "I thought being a girl was really the bunk; I just nearly died," she said.

When she was eight, she came up with a solution to this problem. She announced to her family that from now on they should call her Jimmy. To make herself more credible in the role, she went to the barber and had her long red hair shaved into a crew cut. She continued the practice of shaving her head until she was thirteen.

Overall, Kate's memories of her childhood are utterly happy, even carefree. All this would change, however, the year that Tom died. Kate was fourteen. The circumstances of his death have never been completely resolved.

He and Kate were in New York City visiting with Mary Towle, a close friend of Kit's from Bryn Mawr. Aunt Mary was a favorite of Tom and Kate's. She was brilliant and slightly eccentric, and she loved to take Kit's children for weekends of movies, plays and exploring.

It was Sunday morning, and Kate was sent to the attic room to

Kate and her beloved older brother, Tom. (MOMA)

rouse Tom for their journey back to Hartford. When she entered the room, she saw an odd shadow on the wall. Then she saw Tom, hanging from the rafter by a piece of sheet. He was dead.

She cut him down. With her muscles straining and her heart beating crazily, she managed to place his body carefully on the bed. Then she tore out of the room and out the front door in search of the doctor who lived across the street. Her frantic poundings on the doctor's door were answered by a cook. "My brother's dead," Kate said. "Then the doctor can't help him, can he?" the woman replied as she slammed the door.

Kate at fourteen. (PHOTOFEST)

It seemed impossible to believe that Tom Hepburn, with his stock of family good looks, charm, talents and intelligence, would take his own life at the age of sixteen. But with no other reasonable explanation, Dr. Hepburn told the press that Tom must have been seized by "adolescent insanity." Later, Kate reminded her father of a story he had once told the children. As a student at Randolph-Macon College, Dr. Hepburn had participated in an elaborate and admittedly tasteless prank designed to horrify members of opposing sports teams from northern colleges. They would hire local black men to pose as victims of lynchings. These men knew how to flex their muscles and hold their heads to avoid strangulation. The night before Tom died, Aunt Mary had taken them to see *A Connecticut Yankee in King Arthur's Court*, which features the same prank. Is it possible that Tom had been attempting to try it himself? As Kate says, the family will never know.

The death of a child changes a family forever. And though neither Kit nor Thomas believed in wallowing, the family was devastated. Kate was especially hard hit.

Returning to Hartford's prestigious Oxford School that fall, Kate was no longer an intrepid and lighthearted tomboy. She was withdrawn and alienated. Her grades dropped to the point where she nearly flunked several classes. Her parents pulled her out of school and hired a tutor to teach her at home.

This was a pivotal time for Kate. As she found it increasingly difficult to relate to other young people, she became even more involved with her family. The Hepburns had always been a clannish family. They relished their familial eccentricities and banded together to ward off the rebuffs of their more conservative relatives and neighbors. With Tom's death, Kate became the eldest. Her relationship with her parents changed to one of near equals. They were her confidants and advisors—"two rocks," she calls them. And they would remain so throughout Kate's life, until they each died.

At seventeen, Kate headed off to Bryn Mawr, to carry on her mother's tradition. She would never again be a permanent resident in her parents' household. But throughout her life, even when she was securely ensconced in the Hollywood scene, she considered Hartford and Fenwick her true homes. She returned East frequently, several times a year at least, often much more. Connecticut was (and still is) a respite from celebrity. At Fenwick, she says, she relishes her status as "nothing special."

The young woman who arrived at Bryn Mawr College in 1924 was bright and conspicuous. She was beautiful, although she didn't yet know it, with a sculptured freckled face, unruly red hair, and a body that conveyed both delicacy and power. Her voice was truly unique— a nasal hum tinged with her father's Southern drawl and her mother's metallic New England accent. Many who first met Kate believed she was British.

Despite her magnetic physical presence, Kate felt awkward at Bryn Mawr. Two years of home tutoring had done little to refine her social graces (never Kate's strong suit). Unlike Kit, who had quickly established herself as a nerve center at Bryn Mawr, Kate never really felt that she belonged. On her first evening there, she entered the dining hall looking for a table to seat herself. She made a dramatic entrance wearing a carefully chosen sweater outfit. An older student, observing Kate, referred to her, loudly and sarcastically, as "self-conscious beauty." Though some might have been flattered, Kate considered this a public humiliation. It would be a full year before she entered the dining hall again. She sustained herself on cheap restaurant fare subsidized by her $75-a-month allowance from her father.

Throughout her college years, Kate stuck to the schedule she had developed at home—up at four-thirty A.M. for a cold shower, to bed by nine, exhausted. This didn't allow her much time for late-night bonding sessions with her fellow students.

During her first two years, Kate's academic performance was as dismal as her social life. At one point her grades were so poor that the college wrote to her parents recommending that they withdraw her from school. "If I had a patient in hospitalization, and the patient grew worse, I should not discharge him," replied Dr. Hepburn. "I would try to work out a more efficacious treatment."

Part of the problem was that Kate was pursuing a premed course load that emphasized math and science. Her father loved the idea of his oldest child following him into the profession that had been so rewarding to him. But it quickly became clear that Kate had neither the drive nor the innate math/science smarts to get herself through the premed program. Her grades rose sharply once she switched her major to English.

Better grades meant that Kate was eligible for membership in the drama club, which she immediately joined. She appeared in three plays at Bryn Mawr. Her splashiest role was that of Pandora in an outdoor production of *The Woman in the Moone*, an Elizabethan play. Kate insisted on playing the role barefoot, despite the graveled performance surface. You wouldn't call her an overnight sensation (and neither did Kate). But she made an impression. And she felt encouraged enough to renew her childhood dream of becoming an actress.

Very quickly, these dreams turned into a determined plan. Through a campus contact, she wangled a written introduction to Edwin H. Knopf, the director of a respectable theater group in Baltimore. In February of her senior year, she traveled to Baltimore to present herself to Knopf in person. She did this without telling her family, borrowing the money for the trip from her close (and lovestruck) friend Bob McKnight, an aspiring sculptor who had proposed

(BRYN MAWR COLLEGE)

*Kate as Pandora in the Bryn Mawr
production of* The
Woman in the Moone.
(BEN CARBONETTO)

to Kate earlier in the year (she brushed him off by launching into a monologue about the futility of marriage for artists like the two of them).

In 1941, at the height of Kate's success, Knopf shared his impressions of Kate with *The Saturday Evening Post*. "Her red hair was pulled back into a charwoman's bun. Excitement had blotched her skin under the freckles. Her forehead was wet. Her nose shone," he said. "She was tremendously sincere, but awkward, green, freaky-looking. I wanted no part of her."

After Knopf had sized her up, his objective was to get this oddly intense young woman out of his office as quickly and painlessly as he could. "Write to me when you finish school," he said, quickly turning his attention to papers on his desk.

One of the many concrete pieces of wisdom that Dr. Hepburn offered to his children concerned the art of the pitch. Never make your plea in writing, he said. Always show your face.

So four days before graduation, Kate made another trip to Knopf's office in Baltimore. She sat quietly in the theater for three agonizing hours while Knopf was rehearsing. When he finally noticed her, he was not pleased. But again, he had neither the heart nor the patience to make her understand that she would never be an actress. It would be more trouble to try to dismiss her for good than it would be to give her an insignificant part in his theater troupe. "There are four ladies-in-waiting in *The Czarina*," he said. "Report Monday morning for rehearsal."

Kate waited until after her graduation ceremony to inform her parents of her plans. They had no idea that she was even considering acting as a career. As she predicted, her father was horrified. Like many upstanding citizens of his day, Dr. Hepburn regarded acting as a tawdry profession, not much better than prostitution. He hated any kind of self-promotion. In spite of all of his prestige in Hartford and his involvement with the Social Hygiene Society, he usually managed to keep his name out of the local papers. The idea that his daughter hoped to earn a living as a performer was downright appalling.

On the drive home from Bryn Mawr, Kate and her father battled it out. At one point, Dr. Hepburn threatened to stop the car and take the train home. Kit supported Kate's right to chart her own future. But she remained on the sidelines, interested to see who would prevail.

It was Dr. Hepburn who finally relented. The unity of the Hepburn family would not be sacrificed over a mere career choice. He didn't exactly offer his blessings. But he did give Kate $50, enough money to last a couple of weeks. If she couldn't make it on her own after that, he swore, she had better make other plans.

Despite his outrage, Dr. Hepburn was impressed by his newly grown-up daughter. He had, after all, spent nearly eighteen years teaching her—often by example—how to defend her beliefs. Kate believed she would be a great actress. And though Dr. Hepburn didn't quite understand this, both he and Kit suspected that she wouldn't rest until she had succeeded.

CHAPTER TWO

"I was always fighting fear."

KATE MADE THE TRIP to Baltimore—and her new life—by herself. She was twenty-one years old. It would be her first summer away from Fenwick and the first time she had ventured outside of her family's world. She had made arrangements to stay at Baltimore's Bryn Mawr Club, where she rented a dreary room overlooking an airshaft.

Kate remembers some moments of true anxiety in her first weeks in Baltimore. But overall, she was exuberant. She had a dream. She believed she would fulfill it. And she even had a real job, not an easy feat for a relatively green aspiring actress.

She also had confidence that she had some talent. "I think you either have it or you don't," she says. "Usually if you want to do it very much you can do it. Sometimes you want to do it very much and you can't do it. But I don't think it requires any special brilliance."

Shortly after her arrival in Baltimore, Kate was joined by Bob McKnight, who had graduated from Yale and was biding his time before heading to Rome on a scholarship. The two wound up rooming together at the Bryn Mawr Club—a purely platonic arrangement, despite the fact that McKnight adored her.

Kate was too consumed with her goals to "waste time" on a love

(PHOTOFEST)

affair in Baltimore. Besides, she was attached to another man, a handsome high-society boy she met while she was at Bryn Mawr. Ludlow Odgen Smith ("Luddy") was from a wealthy Philadelphia family. He was sophisticated and educated—schooled in Europe, fluent in several languages, knowledgeable on topics ranging from electrical engineering (his field of study) to music and sailing.

For all of Luddy's talents, though, he was a modest, even passive character. Kate had more charismatic suitors, including Bob McKnight. But no other man fit so neatly into Kate's own life scheme. There was no friction between the two, no clashes of values. With Luddy, Kate always came first. He took her acting plans quite seriously, and never failed to encourage her. And unlike most of her beaux (including Spencer Tracy years later), Luddy appreciated her family. He was a favored guest in both Hartford and at Fenwick.

Kate did not want Luddy's company in Baltimore. "It was all me, me, me," she says. And Luddy was content to wait for Kate to summon him, a mode that would grow quite familiar to him over the next few years.

True to his word, Edwin Knopf had put aside a part for Kate in the upcoming production of *The Czarina*. Perhaps out of guilt for wanting to get rid of her so quickly, he had assigned her the largest of the ladies-in-waiting parts.

But despite this kind gesture, Knopf had no intention of wasting his time nurturing an inexperienced newcomer, especially one that he thought was so clearly unsuited for the stage. Let her have her moment in the limelight, Knopf reasoned. Then let her go home and start a family.

Knopf's company was one of the better stock theater groups in the country. His bigger stars—Mary Boland and Kenneth MacKenna—were well known, and would go on to moderate success in Hollywood.

But if Kate ever felt out of place among her vastly more experienced colleagues, she never let it show. Rather, she projected an air of entitlement and confidence. She settled herself in so quickly that some members of the company were actually taken aback.

Kate zeroed in on Mary Boland right away as the person from whom she could learn the most. During the first weeks of rehearsal, she rarely let the older woman out of her sight. Kate's intense stares unnerved Boland so much that she actually complained to Knopf.

But by the time the curtain went up for *The Czarina*, both Boland and Knopf had changed their minds about Kate's prospects. When Kate was dressed in her costume, when her freckles were tamed by makeup and her hair was placed into an actual style, she was transformed. The only remnants of the scrappy tomboy were in her bright and excited gray eyes. The elegant woman who walked across the stage was sleek and radiant and, as Boland recalled, "borne up by light."

Knopf kept Kate on for his next production, *The Cradle Snatchers*. But it quickly became clear that her voice posed a serious problem. The slightest bit of strain caused it to shoot up an octave and race to unintelligible speeds. She would have to learn to control it, and her colleagues recommended the perfect teacher for the job: Frances Robinson-Duff. Clark Gable and Mary Pickford were just two of the major stars who had benefited from a stint with this flamboyant former actress.

Studying with Robinson-Duff meant leaving Baltimore for New York, a move Knopf urged her to make. He already had plans to open a new play, *The Big Pond*, on Broadway. He promised Kate a supporting role. She would have nine weeks to whip her voice into shape and to prepare for her first important stage performance.

Kate has often given the impression that she simply sailed into acting on a wind of good timing. "I was lucky," she once said. "I was given a wonderful shuffle in the deck. I had wonderful parents, a wonderful family, wonderful friends and wonderful opportunities. I came along at the right time and had the right looks and the right voice."

This is true. Kate was blessed with people to support her. And her look and attitude distinguished her from much of her competition. People tended to remember her, even if they didn't like her. And there were plenty who didn't. Knopf wasn't the only one to initially dismiss her as a hopeless case.

But Kate did pay her dues. Her ego took quite a bashing during the two years she spent trying to establish herself as a stage actress in New York. She was fired from more than half the jobs she was hired for. As she told Charles Higham, "I was what might be called a 'flash actor.' I could read a part without knowing what I was doing better than anyone else in the whole world. I could laugh and cry and I could always get a part quickly—but I couldn't keep it. They got on to me

Kate with Jane Cowl in Art
and Mrs. Bottle, *1930.*
(BEN CARBONETTO)

after a while. I would lose my voice, fall down on lines, get red in the
face, talk too fast, and I couldn't act. The sight of people out there just
petrified me." She clashed with directors and was generally ignored
by reviewers. More than one person tried to convince her to give up.
"I was always fighting fear," she says.

In addition to any innate talent she might have had, Kate had a
priceless asset. She had a certain brand of determination that was
particular to her family—the same quality that got her mother into
Bryn Mawr, helped her father win support for his various crusades,
and compelled Kate to jump into freezing showers every morning of
her life. Despite any doubts she had (which were considerable at
times) she simply behaved—whether alone or in public—as though
she would succeed. More than talent, Kate has said, it was this attitude
that bolstered her through this difficult first chapter of her acting
career.

Frances Robinson-Duff was struck by Kate—taken aback and
impressed. "It was raining," Robinson-Duff recalled of their first

meeting. "She had run up the stairs. She burst in the door, unannounced, and flung herself on that black chest. Rain ran from her red hair and down her nose. She sat in a dripping huddle and stared. 'I want to be an actress,' she said. 'I want to learn everything.'"

Robinson-Duff, of course, had heard this before from countless young hopefuls. "Why did I work with her?" Robinson-Duff claimed, "Sometimes we have an inward vision, a flash. I looked at her, huddled there, bedraggled and wet—at the terrific intensity of that face—and something inside whispered, 'Duse. She looks like Duse.'" Eleonora Duse was a great Italian actress whom Robinson-Duff admired.

During two high-priced lessons per week (Dr. Hepburn had kicked in with more spending money), Robinson-Duff worked to harness Kate's voice and break her of many bad habits. She also tried to influence Kate's personal life, particularly her wardrobe. At the time, Kate went around in a uniform: ratty man's sweaters, baggy pants and coat that she fastened with a large safety pin. "You must dress right," Duff ordered Kate. "You must look like somebody."

What her teacher didn't realize was that Kate did look like somebody. She looked like Kate. As a young woman, Kate had never developed an interest (or even tolerance) for "fussy" feminine adornments, particularly stockings and garter belts. And she never would. Muriel King, who designed Kate's costumes in her 1935 film *Sylvia Scarlett*, once said of Kate, "She can make fashion, but she cannot follow one."

Kate always preferred pants, the baggier the better. When she arrived in New York, she owned just one piece of makeup—an orange-hued lipstick. Her favorite hat was a floppy felt number with a hole in the front. "You won't wear clothes fit for a decent scarecrow, but will you do me a favor?" Robinson-Duff asked. "Throw away that old felt hat and get one without a hole in it."

"Good lord," Kate responded. "What's the matter with people? Can't their imagination supply enough cloth for that little hole?"

She never did change her image. "I have always worn trousers," she once told *Look* magazine, "never not worn them. I know my legs are good, but I marvel that women should be sainted for keeping stockings up. That's one of the most boring tasks that anybody could ever be faced with. I don't wear makeup, not even lipstick."

With Robinson-Duff's help, Kate refined her part in *The Big Pond*.

Kate's taste in clothes appalled her early mentors. Later, though, she became a style-setter. (PHOTOFEST)

But nine days before the play's opening, Edwin Knopf decided to fire his leading lady. Both he and the play's star, Kenneth MacKenna, believed that Kate was better suited for the lead. They also believed that her time with Duff had given her the technique she needed to handle herself on the Broadway stage.

They were wrong. Nine days were barely enough time for Kate to memorize the hefty part and to get a grip on the character. She was left with no time to prepare herself emotionally.

The play premiered in Great Neck, New York. Kate was so nervous that she avoided the theater until fifteen minutes before curtain time. She killed time at the railroad station, sitting on the grass munching on blueberries.

By the time she arrived at the theater, her fellow cast members and the production staff were frantic. She had barely enough time to dress and throw on some makeup. Just as she was about to make her entrance, she realized that the elastic on her panties was too loose. As she rushed on stage, she stopped, quickly removed the underwear, and stuffed them into the hands of a stagehand.

Kate looked wonderful as she made her entrance. One of her first lines was an imitation of a French tour guide, which she delivered flawlessly. But the sound of the audience applauding with approval threw her timing. Her voice ran off without her. For the rest of the play, she raced through her lines in a painful high-pitched buzz. When the curtain finally came down, much of the audience was in a state of punchy relief. Not one of her fellow cast members came to her dressing room following the show.

Kate believed it was important to show the world that she was not beaten by her unfortunate experience in *The Big Pond*. Knopf had asked Robinson-Duff to inform Kate that she was fired from the show. "Look, Miss Robinson-Duff," Kate said after hearing the news. "Aren't you proud of me now? Look how I'm taking it. Not a tear. I don't cry at all."

"I'm not proud of you," Robinson-Duff replied. "How can I make an actress out of you if you keep that shell over your emotions?"

Kate insisted on returning to the theater to say goodbye to the cast of *The Big Pond* and to let them know that she harbored no negative feelings. She also made a trip home, with Luddy in tow, to show her family that she could handle a few knocks.

But Kate was so distressed by this high-profile failure that she decided to leave the stage and marry Luddy. Kate's family was surprised by this decision. Not only had Kate always sworn that she wouldn't marry, but it did not appear that she was actually in love with the man.

But the marriage took place as planned in a quiet ceremony performed by Kate's grandfather. After a honeymoon in Bermuda, Kate and Luddy moved to Philadelphia, where Luddy had a promising job in the insurance industry.

But if Luddy had any illusions about domesticating his new wife, they were short-lived. He even consented to changing his name—his last name—from Smith to Odgen. Kate simply couldn't bear the idea of being known as Kate Smith.

Less than two weeks after they moved, Kate realized she wanted to return to New York. Luddy moved back to New York with her, and the two settled in an apartment on East Forty-ninth Street (where Kate still lives). He provided crucial moral support to her as she tried to jump-start her stage career. "He did everything he could do to make my dreams come true," she says.

But within a few months, they began to lead separate lives. Kate always regretted the way she treated him, calling herself an "absolute pig." "He was an angel," she told Caryn James of *The New York Times*. "I thought of myself first, and that's a pig, isn't it? I think so. He was such a nice man and helped me so much. I was very lucky with Luddy because he really opened door after door after door to me, and I would have been terrified alone in New York City." They would stay legally married until 1935, and close friends until he died. "He and I were friends always. And then when he was older—his wife had died, he had two children—I tried to make up to him for the horror I had caused him. He was so generous-spirited that I don't think he considered it a horror. He just considered it a kid who was wildly ambitious or something." Luddy also remained close to the Hepburn family, who always reserved a third-floor room for him at Fenwick.

As for marriage, Kate would not do it again, nor would she regret her decision not to have children. Being an actor, she resolved, would be her life's work. "Being a housewife and a mother is the biggest job in the world, but if it doesn't interest one, don't do it. It didn't interest me, so I didn't do it. Anyway, I would have made a terrible parent. The first time my child didn't do what I wanted, I'd kill him."

Luddy's role of companion and supporter was soon filled by a vibrant young woman whom Kate met in one of Robinson-Duff's classes. Laura Harding was also an aspiring actress, although she was

The Warrior's Husband, *1932*. (BEN CARBONETTO)

Kate with Laura Harding, a lifelong friend. (MOMA)

far less ambitious than her new friend. She was also the heiress to the American Express fortune. The two were constant companions, and would remain friends for decades.

Kate's flop in *The Big Pond* didn't prevent her from finding other parts. Neither did her reputation as being difficult to work with. Following the Hepburn family policy, Kate always registered her opinions. The fact that a stage direction was being made by a producer or director meant little to Kate, if she happened to disagree. Still, she won small and supporting roles in New York plays and larger parts in regional theaters in New England.

In the winter of 1931, Kate got her second big break: a lead in *The Warrior's Husband*, an update on Aristophanes' *Lysistrata*. Kate was chosen to play Antiope, a female warrior who was to make her entrance by jumping down a flight of steps with a dead deer around her neck. The play's theme—a strong woman tamed by a stronger man—would be echoed later in many of Kate's more successful films, particularly those in which she teamed up with Spencer Tracy.

Kate as Antiope. (BEN CARBONETTO)

L A U R E N   T A R S H I S

The show called for Kate to wear a skimpy costume: a short tunic adorned with metal breast covers. Kate was ideally suited for this physical role. Her years of sports had given her great agility, not to mention nice legs. The play was a hit. And for the first time, reviewers noticed—and praised—Kate's performance. "Miss Katharine Hepburn as the young Amazon Antiope is a boyish, steel-sprung woman who suggests a tougher and more dynamic Peter Pan," wrote the reviewer for the *New York Herald Tribune*.

Kate was intoxicated by her triumph. But she always lamented that her first success came in what she called "a leg show."

(MOMA)

CHAPTER THREE

"*$1500 a week for that?*"

AMONG THE THOUSANDS of people who saw Kate in *The Warrior's Husband* were Stella Bloch and Edward Eliscu, two talent scouts from Hollywood. The day after they saw the performance, Bloch relayed a glowing report back to her childhood friend director George Cukor, and his boss, RKO Pictures' new studio chief, David O. Selznick.

Selznick, a young man with a sharp mind and a reputation as an upstart, had been recruited from Paramount to lift RKO out of a financial sinkhole. The studio had been in business for just two years, but it was already millions of dollars in debt.

Selznick was on the prowl for new talent. At Cukor's urging, he contacted the agent Leland Hayward, who had recently taken Kate on as a client. He told Hayward that RKO was interested in bringing Kate to Hollywood.

Cukor wanted her for his next film: *A Bill of Divorcement*. The studio was set to film this stagey drama about a mentally ill man who returns home from an institution on the day his wife is planning to remarry. John Barrymore was signed for the leading role. Irene Dunne and Carole Lombard were two of the leading actresses hungry for the role of Sydney, the idealistic daughter. But Selznick wanted to cast a newcomer.

Kate agreed to make a screen test for RKO, but she refused to play a scene from the script of *A Bill of Divorcement*. As she told author Garson Kanin: "Everyone seemed to be testing for it and not making it. When I got a chance to test, I looked at the scene, and thought, well, hell, no wonder—the scene's no good—so I made some excuse and said I couldn't do that scene for the test, but would they let me do a scene of my own? They didn't care one way or another."

Kate selected a scene from *Holiday*, the play on which her 1938 hit movie would be based. She had understudied for Hope Williams, the star of the Broadway production the year before. She never got a break (Williams never so much as caught a cold), but Kate did know the part inside out. She knew just how to show herself off.

She asked her co-star from *The Warrior's Husband*, Alan Campbell, to read with her. She sat him well in the back of the frame, barely in camera's view. "I'd seen too many girls make screen tests with juveniles, only to have the juveniles hired," she said.

Kate played the scene with her back to the camera, turning around only in the last moments of the test, when she stared the camera straight on with moist eyes. Kate would have a chance to see the test again in 1938, at a cast party for the film *Holiday*. "The company laughed themselves sick," she said. "I didn't think it was so awfully funny. It's true, I looked terrible in it. But there was something awfully heartbreaking about the girl I was in those days. I was trying so hard—too hard. I was so eager—too eager."

George Cukor loved what he saw in Kate's test. Selznick was less impressed. But after endless prodding by Cukor, he agreed to try to sign her to RKO.

Kate was always happy to be in demand. But she wasn't overly eager to begin the Hollywood phase of her career. She knew that her triumph in *The Warrior's Husband* would lead to any number of interesting opportunities on the stage. She also knew of dozens of promising actors who had gone to Hollywood, only to disappear in the sea of hopefuls.

Selznick and Hayward negotiated for two weeks over Kate's salary. Selznick had opened with an offer of $500 a week—five times more than Kate was earning in *The Warrior's Husband*. Kate insisted that she would accept nothing less than $1500. It was a hefty sum, she knew (not far from the top of RKO's pay-scale). But she wisely figured that the more money RKO had invested in her, the more effort they would make to develop her talent. "There were millions of girls going out West," she said. "I didn't want to be just another one of them."

Kate's parents, who were by this time as excited by Kate's success as Kate was, urged her to stand firm. And Selznick finally did come

HOLLYWOOD IN FLUX

Kate hit Hollywood at a time of radical transition within the film industry—and America. The stock market crash of 1929 and the ensuing Depression had darkened America's mood. Americans wanted to escape to the movies. But the giddy "flapper" pictures that had been so wildly popular just a few years back seemed inappropriate in these somber times. Studios scrambled to find new types of pictures—and new stars—to match this more serious era.

At the same time, talkies had officially killed the silent era—and destroyed some of Hollywood's hottest careers. Gloria Swanson, Pearl White, Colleen Moore, John Gilbert, Clara Bow and director Buster Keaton were just a few of the luminaries who stumbled at the threshold of Hollywood's new era.

Some, like Gilbert, simply had unappealing speaking voices. Others could not adapt to the more subdued, stagey style of acting required for talking pictures. Only a relative handful of silent stars managed to survive—and flourish. Joan Crawford and Greta Garbo are two who made it.

Hollywood talent scouts raided the New York stage for new blood. They looked for actresses who could handle the rigors of talkies, and who radiated intelligence and breeding. Hollywood was still recovering from a decade of sex and drug scandals that came close to destroying the entire industry. The new generation of starlets were to be "ladies," like Carole Lombard and Katharine Hepburn, not vamps like Theda Bara and others who had slithered on the screen a decade before.

Though Hollywood had recovered

Pearl White. (PHOTOFEST)

Clara Bow. (PHOTOFEST)

Joan Crawford in her days as a flapper.
(PHOTOFEST)

(BELOW) John Gilbert. (PHOTOFEST)

from these scandals by 1930, its tawdry edge lingered (and still does). But
even New York's top stage performers
found it difficult to resist the huge sal-
aries offered by the studios. Ethel
Barrymore and Lynn Fontanne both
dabbled in pictures. Ann Harding,
Jeanette MacDonald, Ruth Chatterton
and Miriam Hopkins left the stage for
good.

Katharine Hepburn managed to
keep her career on a parallel course.
Throughout her career, she has had tri-
umphs on both the stage and screen.

GEORGE CUKOR

During the course of his fifty-year career, George Cukor had the chance to direct some of Hollywood's greatest actresses. Greta Garbo, Joan Crawford, Ingrid Bergman, Marilyn Monroe are just some of the legendary figures that passed before his camera.

*But Kate was always his favorite (and Cukor was always hers). They worked together ten times, on some tremendous hits (*A Bill of Divorcement, Little Women, The Philadelphia Story, Adam's Rib*) and one of the era's biggest flops (*Sylvia Scarlett*).*

From the moment they first met, on the set of Kate's first film and their first collaboration, A Bill of Divorcement, *they struck up a kinship that would last until Cukor's death in 1983. Cukor was as well known for his nasty quips as he was for his directing talents. But for Kate, he had only words of love and support.*

Born in New York, in 1899, to Hungarian Jewish parents, he always gravitated toward the arts. A brief and successful career on Broadway brought him to Hollywood in 1928.

*He was known as "a woman's director" for his ability to elicit textured and moving performances from the most recalcitrant leading ladies. Hepburn's Tracy Lord (*The Philadelphia Story*), Judy Holliday's Billie Dawn (*Always Forever*), and Judy Garland's Esther Blodgett (*A Star Is Born*) all came alive through Cukor's magical touch.*

(MOMA)

Kate with George Cukor in 1933, during the filming of Little Women.
(PHOTOFEST)

through. The contract Kate wound up with guaranteed her $1500 per week for four weeks. The studio then would have an option of renewing her contract for five years. Kate was pleased to have won. But the fact that they would offer her so much money only served to reinforce her belief that "Hollywood was full of asses."

Kate brought Laura Harding along for company on the long train ride West. Laura, whose family riches allowed her to do whatever she pleased, had agreed to stick around in Hollywood for a while to help Kate get settled in. The two would room together for two years, until Laura returned to New York.

Halfway through the train ride, Kate stuck her head out of a window for air. As she did, something flew into her left eye. She and Laura tried for hours to flush it out. But it had lodged itself. The eye swelled shut and the other turned bright red—hardly a face she was eager to present to Hollywood.

Their train ride ended in Pasadena, the point of arrival for most of Hollywood's new stars. Leland Hayward and his partner, Myron Selznick, were there to greet them. Kate was wearing a three-hundred-and-fifty-dollar outfit that she had painstakingly selected for her entrance into Hollywood. It was a long navy skirt topped with an elaborate nineteenth-century-style riding jacket ("very odd," Kate would later say). Her hair was pulled back "à la concierge" and her head was topped with a pancake hat. Her face was almost as red as her one open eye.

Selznick and Hayward gaped at Kate as she and Laura made their way down the platform. Selznick turned to his partner and said, "We stuck David for $1500 a week for that?"

Hayward brought Kate directly to the studio to meet Cukor and the cast and crew of *A Bill of Divorcement*. Laura tagged along. But Kate was nervous and her eye was throbbing with pain. As usual, she masked her feelings of insecurity by projecting as many strong opinions as possible. Myron Selznick was the first to be put off. "I was only trying to make conversation!" he snapped at her at one point during their ride to the studio.

Cukor was next. Cukor had tried to break the ice by showing Kate some sketches of the costumes she would wear in the film. "You took out some terrible sketches in order to make conversation, trying to be very sweet," Kate recalled to Cukor in a television appearance they made together in 1969. "And I looked at them, and I said—I thought they were horrible—'Well, I really don't think that a well-bred En-

But whether he was working with women or men like Spencer Tracy, Jimmy Stewart or Rex Harrison, he had a knack for pushing actors further than they thought they could go, always with patience and humor. As he once said, "I choose my actors well and get to know the quirks of their personalities. And most of all, I share humor with them. Then I keep my eyes open when they rehearse and perform, because you never know where the next stimulation comes from."

He was openly homosexual during a time of incredible intolerance in Hollywood. But he was always one of the most popular members of the movie community, a sought-after dinner guest and a favored companion of some of Hollywood's leading figures, male and female. As one Hollywood insider said, "If you showed up to a party with Cukor, instantly, you were somebody."

Kate with her pet gibbon monkey in 1937. (PHOTOFEST)

glish girl would wear anything like that' in a rather prissy way. And you said, 'What do you think of what you have on?' And I was a bit taken aback and I said, 'Well, I think it's very smart,' and you said, 'Well, I think it stinks. Shall we proceed from there?'"

Despite this snippy beginning, Kate and Cukor would become lifelong friends. Even in those first moments, Cukor marveled at how Kate maintained her poise despite his rather nasty remark. He was, after all, the relatively seasoned Hollywood professional. And she hadn't been in town for a full day. "You seemed rather self-possessed," he told her in another joint interview. "All my chiding seemed to just roll off your back. Later you told me that you were quite accustomed to all that . . . from your father."

"Yes," Kate responded. "So I never listened to you. I am sure it's why we got on."

Kate fared a bit better with her co-star, John Barrymore. The acting legend had moved passed his prime, a journey accelerated by his serious drinking problem. But he still had great charm, and had not lost his cachet as a leading man. He greeted Kate with warm praise about her screen test. Then he took her aside to offer her some private counsel and a bottle of eye drops. "I have the same trouble once in a while myself," he said, gesturing to her red and swollen eyes. "A couple of drops into each eye and they'll never know you've been hitting it up."

Kate spent the rest of the day in conferences and hair-dressing and makeup sessions. They chopped her hair, leaving "just enough to curl." She didn't get to see an eye doctor until late that night. After an excruciating hour with a tweezers and a bright flashlight, the doctor extracted three steel filings from her eye. She had to spend the next day wearing an eye patch, which only heightened her feeling that she was an alien in this town.

Kate was, of course, an unusual creature by Hollywood standards. With her sharp features, athletic gait and unrestrained personality, she was clearly not "starlet" material. While most people came to Hollywood eager to fit into established molds—dreamy starlet, flamboyant mogul, dashing leading man—the thought of assimilating never crossed Kate's mind. She only had one persona—strong, independent and brash. It would have to do.

A Bill of Divorcement was shot in five weeks. Despite Kate's inexperience, filming went fairly smoothly. As Cukor has often remarked,

Kate immediately took to the camera. The camera and lighting softened her face while accentuating its dramatic bone structure. And she never felt the awkwardness that stage actors often experience when first working in film. "I remember very accurately the first scene I ever did with Jack Barrymore," Kate has said. "Jack Barrymore came in and was fiddling around with some pipes on the mantelpiece. He had a hat on, and a raincoat, and he turned around and looked at me. I was standing off-camera watching him ... acting away ... full of sincerity, tears streaming down my face."

As Kate recalls, Barrymore approached her and took her chin in his hands. Then he turned to Cukor and asked to reshoot the scene. "He did it again and it was entirely different, much better," Kate recalls. "I think he looked at me and just saw a kid to whom it meant a tremendous amount, and he thought, 'Well, the poor thing, I better do a little better here.'"

A Bill of Divorcement, released in September 1932, was a hit, and so was Kate. *Photoplay* magazine reported that they had never received more letters praising a first screen performance. Virtually every review singled her out. As Richard Watts, Jr., wrote in the *New York*

Kate and Andy Lawler at George Cukor's home, the center of Kate's social life. (MOMA)

With John Barrymore in A Bill of Divorcement, *her film debut, 1932.* (MOMA)

At Cukor's home, with Hugh Walpole and Roly Leigh. (MOMA)

From A Bill of Divorcement. (MOMA)

Herald Tribune: "The most effective portrayal in the film . . . is provided by Miss Katharine Hepburn, who is both beautiful and distinguished as the daughter, and seems definitely established for an important cinema career."

As is true today, one plum role in a successful movie was enough to catapult Kate to the top of everyone's list. Suddenly, everyone wanted to know about her.

Normally, the studio press office would be ready with reams of carefully tailored information about their star. But Kate had made it known in her first days in Hollywood that her private life was not for public consumption. Stardom was one thing. Publicity, as Dr. Hepburn had often insisted, was quite another. "Personally, I'd be very well satisfied if nothing was ever written about me except reviews of my pictures and comments on my work. Because, frankly, I believe the public is interested in me only as an actress, as one who entertains it, and not as an individual," she explained in 1936.

This attitude might make sense in Hartford and Fenwick, but it was considered almost scandalous in Hollywood in the 1930s. Kate's habit of lying to the press didn't help matters. "Do you have any children?" asked one journalist in 1932. "Two white and one colored," Kate replied.

It didn't take long for the usually fawning Hollywood fanzines to lash out at Kate in increasingly bitter articles. "She came to Hollywood a gorgeously 'free soul' kind of person," wrote Sara Hamilton in *Photoplay* magazine in a tone typical of Kate's press in 1933. "And she has simply colored herself, padded her part, heightened her eccentricities for Hollywood. . . . She detached herself from all Hollywood. High on a hill built of her own cunning, she stands. And surveys this Hollywood below her. And imagines her skirts are free of it. At its bewildered groping, she laughs . . . and laughs . . . and laughs. She's smart. She's shrewd. She's clever. But she's forgotten one thing. Hollywood always laughs last. One day she'll find that out."

On the few occasions that reporters were able to corner Kate into answering their questions, her statements were generally clipped and self-righteous. In response to a question about her mother's birth control crusades, she once said: "I detest the newspaper references to her as Katharine Hepburn's mother. My mother is important. I am not."

Kate had three strong showings during her second year in Hollywood. The first was *Christopher Strong*, a weepy drama about a female aviator involved in a forbidden romance with a married man. It was an eccentric movie directed by one of Hollywood's few female directors, Dorothy Arzner, and laced with hints of feminism. While it didn't do as well as *A Bill of Divorcement*, critics continued to lavish praise on Kate. "That troubled, masque-like face, the high, strident, raucous, rasping voice, the straight, broad-shouldered boyish figure—perhaps they may all grate upon you, but they compel

A reporter catches Kate off-guard at Newark Airport. (MOMA)

(ABOVE AND RIGHT) *In* Christopher Strong, *1933.* (PHOTOFEST)

In Morning Glory, *1933.* (PHOTOFEST)

In Morning Glory *with co-star Douglas Fairbanks, Jr., who remains a close friend of Kate's.* (PHOTOFEST)

attention, and they fascinate an audience. She is a distinct, definite, positive personality—the first since Garbo," wrote Regina Crewe of *New York American.*

Kate followed with two more hits. *Morning Glory*, starring Douglas Fairbanks, Jr., was the story of an idealistic actress trying to find success on the New York stage. Kate drew from her own experiences to give a graceful and emotional performance that won her her first Oscar.

Next came one of Kate's personal favorites and her first "classic" film: *Little Women*. Her third movie of 1933 placed her back in the hands of George Cukor. David O. Selznick was involved in the day-to-day aspects of the film, and spared no expense on its production.

On the Morning Glory *set with Lowell Sherman.* (MOMA)

The cast, which included Joan Bennett, Paul Lukas, Enda May Oliver, Frances Dee and Jean Parker, all performed flawlessly. The sets were lavish. And Cukor's touch turned Louisa May Alcott's sugary story into a timeless drama. Even Tallulah Bankhead, who had never been a fan of Kate's, visited the set to watch Kate perform. Bankhead, who used to refer to Kate as a "New England spinster," was overwhelmed when she first saw a clip of Kate's performance. As Kate recalls, "Tallulah came rushing in and she threw herself into my arms and she gave me a big hug and she just burst into tears."

"Katharine Hepburn," wrote *Time* magazine, "is an actress of so much vitality that she can wear balloon skirts and address her mother as "Marmee" without suggesting quaintness. She makes Jo March one of the most memorable heroines of the year, a girl at once eager and puzzled, troubled, changing and secure."

With Cukor during filming of Little Women, *1933.* (PHOTOFEST)

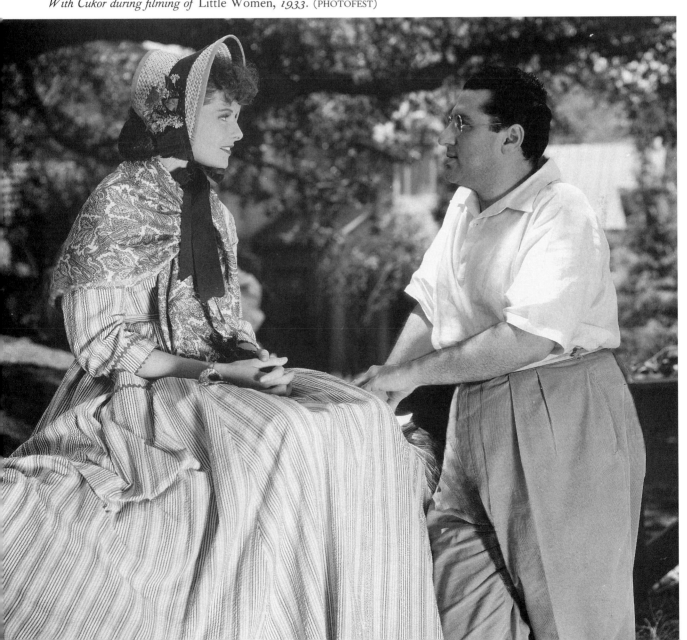

The Little Women *set.* (MOMA)

Lunch on the set of Little Women *was a sumptuous affair.* (MOMA)

(ACADEMY OF MOTION PICTURE ARTS
AND SCIENCES)

KATE   *61*

A HOT ROMANCE: KATE AND LELAND HAYWARD

Not long after Kate's arrival in Hollywood, she became involved in a new romance—with Leland Hayward, one of Hollywood's top agents and most eligible bachelors. In addition to Kate, Hayward's client roster included Helen Hayes, Fred Astaire, Ginger Rogers and writer Ben Hecht.

Hayward was handsome and graceful—matinee-idol material himself. He had a Princeton education and a social pedigree not unlike Kate's. Laura Harding, in fact, had known Hayward during her days on the debutante circuit.

By the time he and Kate became involved, he had earned himself a glittering reputation in Hollywood. Photoplay magazine proclaimed that if Hayward and Kate got married, Hayward would never have to worry about being known as "Mr. Katharine Hepburn. . . . Let us assume Katharine and Leland are married and then say that Leland probably makes more money than his wife, a rare and unusual characteristic of the gents who marry film queens. In fact, it's practically unheard of."

Kate and Hayward were well matched. Both were good-looking, athletic and educated. Hayward, like Kate's close friend George Cukor, was known as one of Hollywood's most sought-after dinner guests. He cultivated a Gatsby-esque image, tooling around in flamboyant cars, flying off in his plane and disappearing for days at a time, and educating himself in a vast array of subjects. He also possessed a kind of strength and decisiveness that reminded Kate of her father.

Kate divorced Luddy in 1934. But

(PHOTOFEST)

she had made it clear that she would not marry again, and that she didn't want children. Still, their affair (which was more like a romantic friendship) continued off and on for several years. And Hayward came closer than any other man to breaking Kate's heart. Their relationship ended late in 1934, when Hayward suddenly and without warning married Margaret Sullavan, another one of his clients. The marriage took place in New York, where Sullavan was performing on Broadway.

Kate was incensed and humiliated when she received word of the marriage. What made the news especially painful was the fact that Sullavan was Kate's rival in Hollywood. The two had similar temperaments and acting styles, and were often pitted against each other in competition for certain roles. Despite their similarities, the two women did not get along. Kate, ever the good sport, sent a telegram to congratulate the couple on their marriage. According to writer Charles Higham, Sullavan ripped it to shreds.

Kate's family and friends barraged Kate with assurances: she could have married Leland if she had wanted to. But it took her many years to get over the sting of what she perceived as a betrayal.

Kate and Leland Hayward.
(BETTMANN ARCHIVE)

Over the course of the year, Kate's relationship with Leland Hayward had taken a romantic turn. By the time *Little Women* was released, the two were one of the most talked-about couples in Hollywood. Since Kate was not legally divorced from Luddy, she did not flaunt their relationship; despite Hayward's taste for nightlife, they were not often spotted out on the town. And they were rarely photographed together.

With the great success of *Little Women*, Kate felt that her standing in Hollywood was secure. Now was the time, she sensed, to make good on a personal promise: to return to New York for a stint on Broadway. She still believed that the theater was where real acting took place. She also wanted to send a signal to Hollywood: that studio star or not, she still controlled her own life and career.

During the filming of *Little Women*, Kate had received a script for the play *The Lake*. It came directly from Jed Harris, a Broadway producer who had once reigned at the very top of the Broadway scene. A string of flops (in addition to a rather obnoxious personality) had threatened his standing in more recent years. Producing Hepburn's return to Broadway would certainly help revive his wobbling career.

The Lake was a melodramatic story of a wealthy young woman coping with the death of her husband—and her one chance at marriage. Harris didn't particularly like the play. But it had succeeded in London, and he thought it might be the right vehicle for Kate. She agreed and made plans to leave for New York immediately.

RKO, however, would not release Kate from her contract, which bound her to one more picture. They had slated her for *Trigger* (later named *Spitfire*), an odd story about a mountain woman who believes that she has the power to heal the sick through prayer. She agreed to work on the film for four weeks for $50,000. Any extra working days, she warned, would cost the studio $10,000 a pop. Filming did run over, and Kate forced the studio to cough up. "I wanted to show them that when we set a definite date, I meant to keep it, even if they didn't. Time means nothing to Hollywood, but it means a lot to me."

When Kate arrived in New York in November 1933, she was met at the train station by a throng of fans. But as she smiled appreciatively at the worshipping crowd, she felt uneasy. Perhaps her mood was a hangover from the tense *Spitfire* set, where she had not gotten along well with director John Cromwell. Or maybe she was upset over the

Spitfire, *1934*. (PHOTOFEST)

on-again-off-again rhythm of her affair with Leland Hayward. But somewhere inside, Kate was nervous. Despite her high hopes, she had the feeling that her return to Broadway was going to be less than triumphant. As she would later recall, she felt like she was taking "a long walk to the gallows."

"... the gamut of emotion from A to B."

KATE KNEW JED HARRIS from her early days in New York. She had auditioned for him several times. And though she was never chosen for one of his productions, she had worked for him briefly, running errands and chauffeuring him around the city in her car. He was attracted to Kate, and wangled an invitation to Fenwick for a weekend with her family, where he was shocked to meet a man whom Kate's mother introduced as "Kate's husband, Luddy."

But any bond they might have forged years before dissolved within the first days of rehearsal for *The Lake*. During the nine days they had to prepare for the play's opening, Harris savagely chipped away at Kate's confidence as an actress. Looking back on those days, Kate readily admits that her acting style was not yet Broadway caliber. But Harris's cruel treatment eliminated any possibility that she might rise to her role. He criticized virtually every aspect of her acting: her voice, her movement, her timing, even her appearance. Kate often wound up in tears.

The dynamics had not improved when the play opened in Wash-

MARTIN BECK THEATRE

THE LAKE

KATHARINE HEPBURN

ington, D.C. Kate has claimed that she "could feel the audience receding" as the play unfolded. She felt awkward and dazed. Harris visited her dressing room afterward to offer his sarcastic reaction. "Perfection," he said. "I can do no more."

Kate knew that her performance was far from perfect. And her instinct was confirmed when the play moved to Broadway a week later. New York's seasoned theater audiences weren't nearly as kind as those in Washington. And critics panned the play. Perhaps the only positive result of Kate's appearance in *The Lake* was that it inspired one of writer Dorothy Parker's more memorable quips: "Katharine Hepburn," she wrote, "ran the gamut of emotion from A to B."

The Lake. (BEN CARBONETTO)

Kate's performance did improve with time; Harris was leaving her alone. By the third week, theatergoers who had read the awful reviews were pleasantly surprised by a measured and moving performance.

But Kate couldn't wait to escape this play. She had to suffer through the fifty-five performances that had been sold out in advance. She also had to deal with rumors that Harris was planning to take *The Lake*—and Kate—to theaters across the country. Initially, Kate dismissed the rumors. But it turned out that Harris was serious, and well within his legal rights. Finally, Kate confronted him over the phone in a conversation that has become famous.

"There's no doubt I stink in the play," Kate remembers telling him. "But nobody was wildly enthusiastic over the production, either. You've got your investment back, and more. Why not call it off? It would be like selling a bottle of patent medicine which you know is no good."

Harris responded with the characteristic warmth of a pool shark. "My dear, the only interest I have in you is the money I can make off of you."

"How much?" Kate asked.

"How much have you got?" Harris responded.

Kate grabbed her checkbook and looked at the balance. "I've got exactly fifteen thousand, four hundred, and sixty-one dollars and sixty-seven cents," she told him.

"Okay," Harris responded, "I'll take that."

Without a second thought, Kate wrote the check. It was a small price to pay for freedom from what endures as her greatest embarrassment. She and Harris never spoke to each other again, although for years following, Harris would bitterly vent his impressions of Kate. To this day, Kate says she does not understand what inspired Harris's cruelty toward her.

Kate remained in New York after *The Lake* closed. She spent her weekdays in her East Forty-ninth Street town house. On the weekends, her new chauffeur, Charlie Newhill (who is still driving Kate around) drove her home to Hartford or Fenwick.

The family dynamic hadn't changed much since Kate went off to college. The atmosphere was still vibrant and chaotic. But her brothers and sisters were grown-up. Both Peggy and Marion had gone to Bennington College. Richard had gone to Harvard and was

Kate with sisters, Marion and Peggy.
(BEN CARBONETTO)

set on a career as a playwright. Robert, also a Harvard graduate, was planning to be a doctor.

Although Kit was now a leader in the birth control movement and traveling the country on speaking engagements, she and the rest of the family devoted plenty of time to helping Kate nurse her wounds and plot the next phase of her career. Unfortunately, no amount of family counsel could have prepared Kate for the next years.

Before returning to Hollywood, Kate hooked up with Laura Harding and traveled to Mexico. It was time to get a formal divorce from Luddy. Her fickle romance with Leland Hayward had heated up again during her run in New York. And she didn't want Luddy to be humiliated by the press coverage, which was becoming more hysterical with rumors (unfounded) of her impending marriage to Hayward.

Although Luddy harbored hopes that Kate would return to him, he accepted her decision to get a divorce. In fact, it had a negligible impact on their relationship, which had already taken the form of a close friendship. They spent time together whenever Kate was in New York. And with or without Kate, he continued to visit Fenwick to spend time with the Hepburns.

The experience of obtaining a Mexican divorce did little to bolster

Kate with Laura Harding in 1934 upon their return from Mexico, where Kate received a divorce from Luddy.

(BEN CARBONETTO)

Kate's mood for her return to Hollywood in the summer of 1934. Still emotionally hobbled from her failure in *The Lake*, she was looking forward to a meaty role to cheer her up. She had been counting on *Joan of Arc*. RKO had already commissioned Thornton Wilder to write the script.

The project was dropped, however, when Wilder couldn't create a script that satisfied the studio. In its place, they pushed Kate into back-to-back failures.

At first, Kate rejected the script for *The Little Minister*, a period piece based on a play by J. M. Barrie. But when she heard that her rival, Margaret Sullavan, was eager for the part, Kate snapped it up for herself. "I really didn't want to play it until I heard another actress was eager for the role," she admitted later.

She would be punished for this.

The Little Minister was a flop. Set in Scotland during the 1840s, the film focused on Lady Babbie, a Scottish aristocrat who disguises herself as a gypsy and falls in love with a rather priggish minister. Even during the brightest times, this homage to spriteness would be annoying. During the Depression, it was intolerable. But critics rather liked the movie, especially Kate's performance. "There is little doubt that the star is one of the major wonder workers of Hollywood, with an unconquerable gift for turning lavender and old lace into something possessing dramatic vitality and conviction," wrote Richard Watts of the *New York Herald Tribune.* Audiences, however, stayed away. And the film lost nearly $10,000. Neither Kate nor the studio fared any better with their next venture, *Break of Hearts.* Most consider this Kate's worst film, and one of the doggiest films to emerge from that era.

These two failures (in addition to *Spitfire*) plagued the conscience of Pandro Berman, who had risen from Selznick's assistant to become RKO's head of production. Berman, who would produce 115 films during his long career (including *Top Hat* and *National Velvet*) would always remain loyal to Kate on a personal level; he enjoyed and admired her. But more than once during their working relationship, he had to confront serious doubts about her bankability. "By this time I realized Kate wasn't a movie star," he recalled of the period follow-

With John Beal in The Little Minister *in 1934.* (PHOTOFEST)

Kate with RKO executive Pandro Berman, who supported her even in tough times. (BEN CARBONETTO)

Break of Hearts, *1935.* (PHOTOFEST)

ing *Break of Hearts*. "She wasn't going to become a star, either, in the sense that Crawford or Shearer were—actresses able to drag an audience in by their own efforts. She was a hit only in hit pictures; she couldn't save a flop. And she almost invariably chose the wrong vehicles."

Berman was able to rescue Kate from the abyss with a script for *Alice Adams*, based on a book by Pulitzer prize–winner Booth Tarkington. The story was a fairly simple small-town drama. But Kate's title role was more textured than any she had previously played.

Alice is a sweet-hearted girl from a poor and troubled family who desperately wants to lift herself to socially higher ground. Her quest is a humiliating one until she meets Arthur Russell (played by newcomer Fred MacMurray), a wealthy young man who is set to marry into the town's most socially prominent family. Despite Alice's clumsiness and low station, he falls in love with her and asks her to marry him.

Kate had initially wanted William Wyler as the director. But the studio suspected that Wyler, a genteel man who was born and raised in Switzerland, would not be able to get into the crevices of this thoroughly American story. Pandro Berman admired the two-reel work of George Stevens, and wanted to give him a chance on a major project. "William Wyler was at that time a very big man in the business," he later recalled. "And George Stevens was still a young man starting out. Katharine and I were sitting together and we couldn't bring ourselves to say either one. So finally I said to her, 'Why don't we flip a coin?' And we did, and it came up Wyler. And I looked at her, and she looked at me, and we both seemed a little disappointed. So I said, 'Shall we flip again?' and we did. And it was Stevens the second time. And we took him."

Kate was attracted to Stevens (most women were). And later on, just before Kate met Spencer Tracy, she and Stevens dated each other quite seriously. But they didn't connect immediately. During the first weeks of shooting, Stevens and Kate were constantly testing each other. His pensive style (he would ponder a shot for hours while his actors stood waiting) drove Kate crazy. And he didn't seem to appreciate her more effusive nature.

Gradually, though, Kate came to respect Stevens's instinct and Stevens began to admire Kate's strong opinions about her character.

GEORGE STEVENS

George Stevens began his movie career in 1927, when Hal Roach hired him as a cameraman for his two-reel slapstick comedies. He was soon directing his own short films, and with the advent of sound, his first feature film: Alice Adams.

Over the course of his career he would direct twenty-five films, including Woman of the Year, Talk of the Town, Gunga Din, I Remember Mama, A Place in the Sun, Shane, *and* Giant. *Kate and Stevens were dating in 1941, prior to the filming of* Woman of the Year. *He was one of the first to notice the attraction between Kate and Spencer Tracy and is said to have gracefully stepped aside as their romance blossomed.*

As a director, he was known to work slowly. His fastidiousness was a constant source of annoyance to his producers (after 1938, he produced his own films). But he was able to elicit from his actors some of the screen's most thoughtful, inward performances.

An assignment to photograph Nazi death camps during the liberation affected him deeply. Because of his realization that the war had brought an end to America's innocence toward the world, Stevens's post-war films contained a troubling complexity and cynicism. He is perhaps best remembered for his films of that era: A Place in the Sun, Shane, *and* Giant—*his "American Trilogy."*

Stevens's career ended tragically in 1965. His movie of that year, The Greatest Story Ever Told, *was a singularly spectacular financial and critical disaster. He never recovered.*

The breakthrough came at the end of the third week, during a scene that called for Alice to burst into tears in her bedroom. The script required Alice, who believes she has lost a rare chance for love, to enter her room, flop onto her bed, and burst into tears. Although they had followed the script in rehearsals, Stevens suggested that Kate play the scene more subtly. He wanted her to walk slowly to her window, and to begin to cry as she looks out at the rainy night.

"I'll cry on the bed," Kate said sharply. "That's how we rehearsed it."

They argued for four hours. "Miss Hepburn," Stevens finally said, sucking on his ever-present pipe. "Just walk to the window, please, and stand there a while. You needn't weep. I'll dub someone in, in a long shot, and we can fake the sound track." Kate, jolted by the insult, walked to the window and cried on the first take.

Stevens's constant but gentle prodding helped Kate create a thoroughly sympathetic Alice. Miraculously, Alice's frantic social climbing never seems ridiculous or distasteful. And the film's small-town flavor was just the thing for Depression-era audiences. Released in 1935, *Alice Adams* actually made money for the studio, and briefly restored RKO's faith in Kate. It also earned Kate her second Oscar nomination. She lost out to Bette Davis.

Any joy that Kate felt over the success of *Alice Adams* was dampened by the final ending of her affair with Leland Hayward. Their romance had been waning for months; Hayward rarely dropped by the set of *Alice Adams*, and he had seemed more and more absorbed in the careers of his other clients. Kate was at Cukor's house when she was shocked to receive word of his marriage to Margaret Sullavan.

Compounding Hayward's betrayal was Laura Harding's decision to leave Hollywood and return to the East Coast. She was fed up with the Hollywood life, and she was feeling increasingly superfluous in Kate's. It was time, she later said, to start living for herself. Kate understood Laura's perspective. She never felt particularly at home in California, either. In all the years she worked in Hollywood, she never bought her own home. She always rented, usually moving to a new abode each year.

With Fred MacMurray in Alice Adams. (PHOTOFEST)

On the Alice Adams *set.* (MOMA)

CHAPTER FIVE

"The most completely honest woman I've ever met."

THRILLED BY THE SUCCESS of *Alice Adams*, Pandro Berman gave Kate free rein—and a blank check—to choose her next film. She went straight to Cukor and they decided to pursue one of their dream projects: *Sylvia Scarlett*. Based on a Scottish novel, the story focused on an emotional triangle between a young woman, her slightly corrupt father and a dashing con-man, who would be played by Cary Grant. The story called for Kate to spend much of the film disguised as a man, an interesting challenge for any actress, but especially appealing to Kate, who still felt like a tomboy at times.

Production moved forward quickly, and the atmosphere on the set was playful, even joyous—Cukor's snippy jokes, sumptuous food, great chemistry between Kate and Cary Grant.

Kate, disguised as a man in Sylvia Scarlett. (MOMA)

In Sylvia Scarlett. (PHOTOFEST)

Berman had hated the script for *Sylvia Scarlett*. But he ignored his instincts and poured nearly $1 million into the film, an enormous sum. But both Kate and Cukor soothed his worries by acting with extreme confidence. Cukor went around saying that *Sylvia Scarlett* would be the biggest hit of his directing career.

Much later, both Cukor and Kate admitted that they experienced serious personal doubts during filming. And in retrospect, it's tough to imagine how either Kate or Cukor could have imagined that *Sylvia Scarlett* would fly in 1935. The story is fascinating today. But it's almost amusing to imagine how audiences would have reacted to the potent and confusing sexual overtones that dominate much of the story.

Any lingering thoughts of a hit movie were crushed during one of the early screenings, when Cukor and Kate sat in the audience and registered people's reactions. "Why aren't people laughing?" Kate whispered to Cukor during one comic scene. "Because they don't think it's funny," he said. "The way the audience looked at us," he said later, "I felt as if we were being stoned."

Kate and Cukor begged Berman to simply scrap the film. They offered to do another project for free, immediately. RKO kept the movie hidden on its shelves for a couple of months. But Berman decided it was too expensive to just throw away. They released it. Critics panned it. And the studio lost more than $300,000.

There was, however, one bright spot in the release of *Sylvia Scarlett*: the launching of Cary Grant as a comic actor. Kate worried that the film's disastrous showing would hinder Grant's burgeoning reputation as a screen idol. But even the harshest critics praised his performance.

Sylvia Scarlett was the first of four films in which the two starred together. Only one of their films, *The Philadelphia Story,* would be a hit when it was first released. But today, *Bringing Up Baby* and *Holiday* are also considered classics.

Kate and Grant never became intimates; Grant was charming but remote. Nevertheless, they always enjoyed working together, and their quippy, physical styles made them natural screen partners. "As an actress she's a joy to work with," Grant once said of Kate. "She's in there trying every moment. There isn't anything passive about her; she 'gives.' And as a person, she's real. There's no pretense about her. She's the most completely honest woman I've ever met."

Kate lunching with love Howard Hughes on the set of Sylvia Scarlett. (ACADEMY OF MOTION PICTURE ARTS AND SCIENCES)

Howard Hughes taught Kate how to pilot a plane. (ACADEMY OF MOTION PICTURE ARTS AND SCIENCES)

Shortly after the release of *Sylvia Scarlett*, Kate embarked on the second serious romance of her Hollywood days. Howard Hughes was one of America's few non-Hollywood celebrities. At thirty-two, he was as famous for his adventures as an aviator as he was for his massive wealth. Like Leland Hayward, he was flamboyant and handsome, and one of America's most eligible bachelors.

Kate had heard that Hughes was angling to meet her throughout the filming of *Sylvia Scarlett*. But she had little interest in meeting a man who seemed to invite the kind of fawning press attention that she herself shunned. When he finally showed up on the set for lunch (he was a friend of Cary Grant's) she did her best to ignore him.

Not easily deterred, Hughes spent the next few months strategizing

Exclusive! COMPLETE GUIDE TO ANSWERS IN $250,000 MOVIE QUIZ

Modern Screen

THE LARGEST CIRCULATION OF ANY SCREEN MAGAZINE

NOVEMBER 10 CENTS

WILL AMERICA'S HERO, HOWARD HUGHES, *Marry* KATHARINE HEPBURN?

Hedy Lamarr's LIFE STORY!

ways to capture Kate's attention. He once even landed his plane on the Beverly Hills golf course where Kate was playing. It took a team of mechanics to disassemble the plane and remove it piece by piece from the course.

His campaign of courtship finally paid off in Boston, where Kate had gone to appear in a stage production of *Jane Eyre*. He checked himself and his entourage into her hotel (and onto her floor) and attended all of her performances. At last, she succumbed. "I must have been lonely," she later admitted. "But he was hard to resist."

Hughes accompanied her across the country as she finished her run of *Jane Eyre*. They returned to California together and Kate moved into his Beverly Hills home. The two passed their days golfing and flying up and down the California coast, often with Kate at the controls (he taught her how to fly). The papers practically hummed with rumors of marriage.

Kate's affair with Hughes was a merciful distraction from what was a fairly depressing chapter in her career. Following the failure of *Sylvia Scarlett*, Pandro Berman and his colleagues at RKO were desperate to figure out how to make use of Kate. Flops or no flops, she was still one of RKO's most valuable stars, especially since Irene Dunne and Constance Bennett had left the studio.

But the studio couldn't seem to come up with material that would appeal to Depression-era audiences. "We really hadn't found the right image for her," Berman said. Rather than learning their lesson from the success of *Alice Adams*—a small-scale American story— Berman and his studio colleagues kept dressing Kate up in overblown historical sagas.

Mary of Scotland, released in 1936, was the first of these. Berman had seen the production on Broadway, and he imported it to Hollywood especially for Kate. The production couldn't have been more beautiful, with sets that were historically accurate down to the last

As Mary of Scotland, 1936.
(PHOTOFEST)

A COLLAGE OF IMAGES

Who is Hepburn? Is she the next Garbo? An ingenue? A sex kitten? Hollywood's image makers transformed Kate into dozens of different images during her first years in Hollywood. She proved to be quite versatile. But it wasn't until Stage Door, *in 1937, when she played her first "rich, arrogant girl" that she settled on the intelligent and tailored image that was all hers, and that would take her through the next phase of her career.* (THIS PAGE, TOP RIGHT, PHOTOFEST; ALL OTHERS, MOMA. OPPOSITE PAGE, TOP RIGHT AND BOTTOM LEFT, PHOTOFEST; TOP LEFT, BEN CARBONETTO; OTHERS, MOMA.)

With Herbert Marshall in A Woman Rebels, *1936.* (MOMA)

In Quality Street, *1937.* (ACADEMY OF MOTION PICTURE ARTS AND SCIENCES)

table leg, and with Kate gussied up in lavish costumes designed by Walter Plunkett.

But with a rather soggy story and a weak script, the film required the perfect director, someone who would help the actors—especially Kate—call forth the spirits of their sixteenth-century characters. John Ford, who had already established himself as the king of Westerns, could not have been a poorer choice. Kate adored Ford. But the tobacco-chewing Irish-American wasn't known for his sensitivity toward women. And he had little sense of how to coax a strong performance from Kate, particularly when her character—a queen— was so far afield from anything he had ever encountered.

Kate enjoyed working on the film. She particularly enjoyed performing her own stunts on horseback. During one of her more elaborate routines, Ford saw her galloping at full speed, seemingly oblivious to a branch that was jutting out in her path. "Duck!" he yelled. Kate obeyed, crunching her head into her chest, and avoiding almost certain decapitation.

Even Kate's most admiring critics had trouble sugar-coating the tedious *Mary of Scotland*. "Katharine Hepburn often acts like a Bryn Mawr senior in a May Day pageant," noted the critic for *Time*.

Still, the studio plowed forward with two more period films: *A Woman Rebels* and *Quality Street*. Both were dreary failures.

As her career sank under the weight of all of this poorly chosen material, her affair with Hughes continued. She discovered that she actually enjoyed being part of the whirl of publicity that his adventures inspired. When Hughes set out to break the speed record for a solo flight over the Atlantic, Kate was delighted to receive daily reports of his progress.

In early 1937, Kate was finally presented with a promising script: *Stage Door*, based on the play by Edna Ferber and George S. Kaufman. The story was definite hit material—perfect for the times and perfect for Kate. It was set in the Footlights Club, a slightly seedy but homey rooming house for aspiring actresses in New York. Cluttered with snappy banter and appealing personalities, the play interwove the stories of several young women, all pursuing their dreams of success on the stage.

Kate played Terry Randall, an arrogant debutante who moves into the Footlights for the chance to experience "real life." At first, her breeding and obvious wealth alienate her from the rest of the girls,

With Lucille Ball and Ginger Rogers in Stage Door. (MOMA)

With Ginger Rogers. (ACADEMY OF MOTION PICTURE ARTS AND SCIENCES)

particularly her roommate, a brassy small-town blonde. But with time, Terry earns the respect and friendship of her housemates, and a Broadway triumph of her own.

Kate was shocked to find out that the studio was not planning to give her top billing in *Stage Door*. That honor would go to Ginger Rogers, who had been hired to play Kate's roommate. Rogers's partnership with Fred Astaire had made her RKO's top-grossing female star. Her addition to the cast of *Stage Door* sent Kate a clear message: RKO had lost faith in her. She could no longer be depended upon to "carry" a picture.

To make matters worse, the studio initially wanted to give Kate third billing, after Rogers and the male lead, Adolphe Menjou. She complained to Pandro Berman, who responded, only half-joking, "You'd be lucky if you played seventh part in a successful picture." During rehearsals, when it was clear that Kate was emerging with a wonderful performance, Berman changed his mind and put Kate at the top of the credits.

Stage Door grossed nearly $2 million. It was a major success for the studio, for Kate, and for Ginger Rogers, who was effectively launched as a dramatic actress. But even more significant, *Stage Door* established Kate's most successful image, one that she would come to call her "rich, arrogant girl."

Heartened by Kate's success in a comic role, Pandro Berman decided it was time for Kate to try a screwball comedy, the brash physical style of comedy that had been earning millions for other studios. Like Irene Dunne, Claudette Colbert and Carole Lombard, the queens of screwball, Kate projected the kind of intelligence, charm and breeding that these films relied on to balance out their often ridiculous plots.

RKO cast Kate in *Bringing Up Baby*, the story of a rich and flaky young heiress, a clumsy paleontologist and an unruly pet leopard, named Baby. Cary Grant was cast opposite Kate, and Howard Hawks was brought in to direct.

Kate enjoyed working on this movie. Unlike her colleagues on the set, she was unfazed by the presence of Nissa, the rather unfriendly leopard who played Baby. She gamely followed the trainer's advice on working with the big cat, regularly dousing herself with a perfume that, according to the trainer, calmed Nissa's nerves. The trainer told a reporter that if Kate should ever choose to drop out of acting, she would make a fine animal trainer. She had the right mix of sympathy and nerve.

Today, many critics consider *Bringing Up Baby* to be the paradigm of the screwball genre. And it's a favorite among this generation of Sunday afternoon classic movie buffs. But when it was released in 1938, the film floundered after a promising opening in New York. Audiences across the rest of America, apparently, had had their fill of screwball comedies. And critics were at best lukewarm. "To the Music Hall yesterday came a farce which you can barely hear above the precisely enunciated patter of Miss Katharine Hepburn and the ominous tread of derivative gags," wrote Frank Nugent of *The New York Times*. RKO lost $365,000 on the film.

The failure of *Bringing Up Baby* would be only the mildest trial that Kate would face in 1938. Just a few weeks after the film's release,

With director Howard Hawks and Cary Grant during the filming of Bringing Up Baby, *1938.* (ACADEMY OF MOTION PICTURE ARTS AND SCIENCES)

Kate had a way with Nissa, the leopard who played "Baby." (ACADEMY OF MOTION PICTURE ARTS AND SCIENCES)

Relaxing with Cary Grant.
(BEN CARBONETTO)

Harry Brandt, president of the powerful Independent Theatre Owners of America, took out an advertisement in a Hollywood trade paper. In it was the list of stars who Brandt and the members of his association considered "box-office poison." Kate headed the roster that included Joan Crawford, Greta Garbo, Fred Astaire, Mae West, and Marlene Dietrich, among others. The list made for colorful headlines in papers across the country. "They say I'm a has-been," Kate said. "If I weren't laughing so much, I might cry."

Brandt's nasty gesture was a blow to all of the stars he listed, but to Kate in particular. If her string of flops hadn't already shaken RKO's faith in Kate (not to mention her reputation with the public), her top-of-the-poison-list status destroyed any remnant of confidence Pandro Berman and the others might have had in her.

Kate avoided a confrontation with RKO by loaning herself out to Columbia Pictures to play in *Holiday*, in the role she had understudied on Broadway nearly ten years before. Her character, Linda Seton, is a New York City heiress who tries to salvage a love affair between her

With Doris Nolan and Cary Grant in Holiday, *1938.* (PHOTOFEST)

More than any other role,
Holiday's *Linda Seton matched*
Kate's real-life persona.
(PHOTOFEST)

sister and a dashing non-conformist named Johnny Case. In the process, Linda falls madly in love with Case, and winds up joining him on an extended "holiday" of self-discovery and adventure. The film gave Kate the chance to work again with two of her favorites: George Cukor and Cary Grant.

Perhaps more than any other role in Kate's early career (even *The Philadelphia Story*, which was written for her) *Holiday*'s Linda was perfectly tailored to Kate's personality. Hard-edged but soft-hearted, Linda has just the sort of cut-to-the-bone intelligence that people have always admired in Kate. *Holiday* stands as one of Kate's finest and most appealing performances.

But once again, Kate's performance was wasted—yet another victim of bad timing. Depression-era audiences could not relate to the idea of Johnny Case shunning a promising and lucrative career in banking to head off on his "holiday." Most found the movie's premise ridiculous and insulting since many Americans were desperate for work of any sort.

When Kate returned to RKO, she was greeted with a script for a film called *Mother Carey's Chickens*, which had all the markings of a B picture. Kate saw that RKO wanted her out of its stable. And she decided to go gracefully, even though it meant that she had to buy out her contract for nearly $200,000. She would never again work for RKO.

Kate packed her bags and returned East, just in time for summer at Fenwick. In the company of her family, Laura Harding and Luddy, Kate filled her days with golf and tennis, walks along the beach and frequent swims in the Long Island Sound. She quickly fell back into the brisk but calming rhythm of her family's life. Numerous offers came from Hollywood, all fairly cut-rate. Paramount sent a script and an offer for $10,000 a picture, down from the $150,000 she was earning at RKO.

Kate held out some hope that her career would be resuscitated by the role of Scarlett O'Hara, which David O. Selznick had been trying to cast for the better part of the year. She had been pining for the role for two years, since she read Margaret Mitchell's book at the suggestion of RKO's talent scout. Kate urged the studio to pick up the film rights. But Berman considered its $56,000 price tag too high for a role the studio considered "unsympathetic."

Since Selznick had bought the rights for MGM, Kate had been

lobbying for the part. Selznick liked Kate, and told her he would keep her on the short list (along with Paulette Goddard, Joan Bennett, Jean Arthur and Loretta Young). But he also let her know that he had serious doubts about casting her. Kate insisted on knowing why. "Frankly," he told her, "I can't imagine Clark Gable chasing you for ten years."

"Well, David," Kate responded, "some people's idea of sex appeal is different from yours."

Kate found out that Vivien Leigh had been cast as Scarlett in September 1938. She had little time to mourn. On September 21, Fenwick was thrashed by one of the most powerful hurricanes in New England's history. Winds soared to nearly two hundred miles per hour. The normally flat Long Island Sound frothed with enormous waves. Kate, Kit and her brother Richard were the only ones home as the skies darkened. They had no idea what was in store. Kate, delighted by the rough surf, took a dip.

By the time they realized what was happening, they were almost trapped by the rising waters. They escaped through a dining-room window about fifteen minutes before the sixty-year-old house was swept off its foundation and into the seas. "I remembered this beautiful gold clock that Howard Hughes had given me, and I rushed upstairs to get it," Kate said. "But halfway up, I thought, 'What the hell am I doing worrying about a gold clock when my mother might be about to drown?' So I tore back downstairs again without it, and no one else ever found it. At least no one said they did."

The Hepburns reacted to their tragedy with predictable style. They spent a few days digging around the property for valuables (they recovered most of the family silver), and prepared to rebuild, on the same spot. Kate went to FAO Schwarz in New York City and purchased a set of child's blocks, which the family used to design the new house. Construction began just weeks later, and the house was finished before the next summer. It still stands.

As she settled into her life on the East Coast, it became increasingly clear to Kate that her relationship with Howard Hughes was ending. Despite their good chemistry, Kate had long sensed that the relationship was doomed. She never believed that two such independent souls could endure as a couple. Their affair never officially ended. It simply evolved into a close friendship that lasted many years.

"Another rich, arrogant girl."

ARLIER IN THE SUMMER, Kate had received a call from the playwright Philip Barry, who had been working on two plays with Kate in mind. Like Kate, Barry had suffered through a string of flops, and was looking for the right vehicle for a graceful comeback.

Kate invited him to Fenwick, and they spent the afternoon discussing Barry's two ideas. One of them was called *The Philadelphia Story*. Barry described the play as the story of a wealthy young woman whose second wedding is disrupted by a couple of tabloid reporters. With Kate's pledge of interest, Barry returned to his home in Maine and tried to bring his idea to life.

One day before the hurricane, Kate received Barry's first act. She loved it. The lead character, Tracy Lord, was "another rich, arrogant girl." Like Terry Randall in *Stage Door*, Tracy is redeemed at the end of *The Philadelphia Story*. A weekend of witty banter and social chaos is enough to show her the "human being" that dwelled inside her icy facade.

Barry had an uneasy time evolving the play into a finished draft. Indeed, years later he would say he was never satisfied with it. But Kate believed it was worthy of Broadway. And the Theater Guild,

which had produced the production of *Jane Eyre* in which Kate starred, agreed. The Theater Guild did not have enough money to finance the production, so Kate kicked in with some funding, and Howard Hughes (still devoted though they were no longer romantically involved) contributed the rest.

The play opened in New Haven in February 1939. The audience seemed to love it, but Kate was nervous that she had misjudged the quality of the play. She went so far as to ask the Theater Guild to withdraw it from the Broadway track. The Guild refused.

As they prepared for New York, Barry labored to refine the play and Kate worked (often with her old coach Frances Robinson-Duff) to iron out her performance. She was nearly unhinged by her nerves during the days preceding the Broadway opening; her memories of *The Lake* plagued her.

The play's opening scene placed Kate alone on stage, arranging flowers in a vase. On opening night, as she stood in position before the curtain went up, she braced herself for another fiasco. She tried to calm herself by muttering to herself, "This is Indianapolis, not New York," over and over.

But as the curtain went up, Kate relaxed into the role and lit up the play as Barry had never seen it before. Audiences loved it. Critics

(PHOTOFEST)

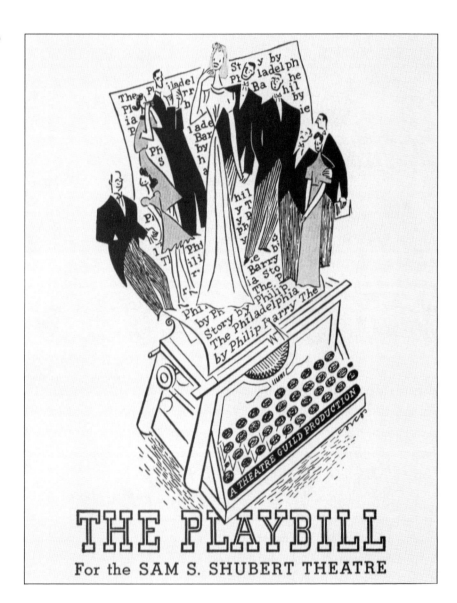

On Broadway in The Philadelphia Story *with Vera Allen and Dan Tobin.* (BEN CARBONETTO)

loved it. It played for 415 performances in New York and 250 on its tour around the country. All told, it grossed nearly $1,750,000. *The Philadelphia Story* not only saved Kate's career—since she owned one-fourth of the production, it made her a fortune.

Howard Hughes had bought Kate the film rights for *The Philadelphia Story* well before the play opened. If the play was a hit, Hollywood was sure to snap it up. But as Kate knew, few studios would be willing to gamble on her as the star of the big-budget film—unless they had no choice. Her ownership of the film rights ensured that no one but Kate would ever play Tracy Lord on the screen.

Within days of the New York opening, Kate was fielding offers from Hollywood. She chose MGM because she respected Louis B. Mayer. She cut the deal herself. Although Leland Hayward was still officially her agent, she liked negotiating for herself (another habit ingrained by her father).

LOUIS B. MAYER

Walter Pidgeon liked to tell a story about the time he approached his boss, Louis B. Mayer, for a raise and contract renewal. The two were chatting about their common hometown when the topic of Pidgeon's salary came up. "Louis, I'm going to leave this in your hands. As a hometown boy, I know you'll do right by me." No sum was ever mentioned, but when his next paycheck arrived, it was twice what Pidgeon had expected to receive.

Such acts of generosity were typical of the man known to his friends as L. B. or Louis, the man who created the world's most exciting and successful studio: Metro Goldwyn Mayer (MGM).

In its heyday in the thirties and forties, MGM produced and distributed a bumper crop of smashes that embodied the magic of the old movies: Pride and Prejudice, Camille, Mrs. Miniver, The Philadelphia Story *and* Gone With the Wind, *to name just a few. Under the management of the flamboyant Mayer, the studio's extravagant, lush productions bore his unmistakable stamp.*

Known to treat his stars better than any studio head, Mayer attracted such luminaries as Clark Gable, Spencer Tracy, Norma Shearer, Greta Garbo, Jean Harlow, Joan Crawford, Robert Montgomery, Myrna Loy and Kate— as well as great directors like King Vidor, Victor Fleming, George Cukor and Clarence Brown.

A fine actor himself, Mayer would use any method necessary—threats, cajolery, insult, bribery, even tears—to win an argument. His histrionics were legendary; Mayer was known to drop to his knees for impact. During the Depression, he was able to convince his employees to take a 15 percent pay cut

(PHOTOFEST)

Mayer offered her $175,000 for the film rights, a generous sum. He tried to talk her out of starring in it, but eventually relented and gave her an additional $75,000 as an acting fee. Kate always particularly enjoyed her dealings with Mayer, whom she considered tough but fair and always engaging. "Louis B. Mayer tried to make a tricky deal with me," Kate recalled of her bargaining sessions with him over *The Philadelphia Story*, "wanting to put Norma Shearer or somebody else in it, and I said, 'Look, Mr. Mayer, I know you are deliberately trying to charm me, and yet I'm charmed,' and he came to a very fine arrangement, with me getting my own way. . . . After Mr. Mayer and I worked out my contract, I went downstairs to his lawyer and said, 'You couldn't very well cheat me, because you're Louis B. Mayer's lawyer. That would be a terribly dishonest thing to do.'"

During her talks with Mayer, she told him that she wanted Spencer Tracy and Clark Gable as her co-stars. Mayer doubted either would accept. But at Kate's request, he asked them both. When they declined, he suggested Jimmy Stewart for the role of Mike Connor, the tabloid reporter and Tracy Lord's fleeting love interest. Stewart accepted. Mayer then gave Kate $150,000 to find an actor to play Tracy's ex-husband, who also shows up on her wedding weekend.

Hepburn wanted—and got—Cary Grant. Mayer also gave her the freedom to choose her director. Naturally, she hired George Cukor.

Cukor had just eight weeks to film *The Philadelphia Story*; shooting was sandwiched between the end of the Broadway run and the beginning of the national tour. But despite the hectic pace, the atmosphere on the set was friendly and relaxed. Kate felt immediately at home on the MGM lot, where actors were pampered as members of Louis B. Mayer's "extended family." Kate hung back on the set, allowing Cukor to take control while she enjoyed the exciting atmosphere of a sure hit in the making. She willingly surrendered star billing to Cary Grant; his contract stipulated that he receive top billing, and Kate figured that it could only help the film.

The Philadelphia Story broke box-office records for 1940. Kate, Grant and Stewart were all nominated for Academy Awards, and Stewart took home the Oscar for Best Supporting Actor. With the tremendous success of *The Philadelphia Story* (on both the stage and screen) Kate again had some clout in Hollywood.

It also marked a turning point in the way she handled her career. Never again would she have a multi-deal contract at the studio. She and Mayer had a verbal agreement that she would stick with MGM (and she kept it for ten years, until Mayer was forced out of MGM). But she would never again legally bind herself to one organization. Neither would she let others choose her material for her. Her success with *The Philadelphia Story* proved that she needed to play an active role in seeking out and developing her own vehicles.

(gladly) when other studios were only asking for 10 percent.

Mayer saw his employees as members of his extended family, and although the punishment for disloyal behavior was severe, the rewards were often tremendous. Mayer showered his favorite stars with high pay, extravagant gifts and great roles. His publicity department would go to great lengths to bail out those in trouble, cover up scandal, and keep career-breaking transgressions from the press. He was rewarded for his attentions by a loyalty that is remarkable for the film business. Many of his workers, at all levels, stayed with the studio for their entire careers.

In 1951, Mayer was ousted from MGM by his own second-in-command, Dore Schary. His homey management style was considered out-of-date, as were his "family pictures." It was the end of a career, and also an end to the movies' most magical era.

On stage with Dan Tobin, Joseph Cotton, Van Heflin, and Shirley Booth. (BEN CARBONETTO)

Filming The Philadelphia Story, *1940.* (PHOTOFEST)

Overall, she seemed to be at peace with Hollywood. She had little interest in serious romance, but engaged herself in an enjoyably light romance with director George Stevens. The familial atmosphere on the MGM set—with its paternal publicity department, its comfortable dining rooms, and the relentless support of Louis B. Mayer—made her feel safe and protected. Although she didn't drop her tight hold on her privacy, she did soften her approach to the press. In several interviews, she actually apologized for her "bratty" behavior of the past. Gossipmonger Louella Parsons reported that there was a "new and mellower Katharine Hepburn."

Kate's next film, *Woman of the Year*, was conceived by Ring Lardner, Jr., a young screenwriter whose father was the legendary sportswriter. He wanted to write a script loosely based on the life of Dorothy Thompson, a high-powered and sophisticated political columnist who had dated Lardner Sr.

He suggested the idea to Garson Kanin, another writer and a close friend of Kate's. Kanin was heading off to the army, but he helped Lardner plump up the idea and hooked him up with his younger brother, Michael. Once the two had a finished treatment, Kanin sent it over to Kate.

Kate adored the treatment, and spent the next few weeks working feverishly with Kanin and Lardner to smooth it into a final draft. *Woman of the Year* featured a Thompson-like character named Tess Harding, a brilliant and beautiful international-affairs columnist who is unbelievably well-connected for such a young woman. She is forever dashing off to various corners of the globe to meet with world leaders and dignitaries who value her for both her intelligence and friendship.

Her life hits a snag when she falls in love with a coarse but sweet sportswriter named Sam Craig. After a brief courtship, the two marry. But very quickly it becomes clear that Tess's career does not allow for the kind of marriage and companionship that Sam expects. Can this marriage be saved?

Kate sent the treatment to MGM without including the names of the authors. She knew that Mayer would never pay top dollar for a script penned by relative unknowns. When Joseph Mankiewicz, MGM's executive producer, asked Kate who wrote it, she replied simply that it was "a secret."

Within twenty-four hours of dropping the script off at MGM, Kate was meeting with Mankiewicz and Mayer. Kate started to talk as soon as she sat down. She would love to bring this picture to MGM, she said. But she would not haggle over prices. If Mayer wanted *Woman of the Year*, he would have to pay $100,000 for her to star, $50,000 for each of the writers, plus $10,000 for agent fees. "And," she added, "I'll only sell it to the studio if you can get Spencer Tracy."

Kate left the two men to talk alone. Minutes later Mankiewicz found her and planted a kiss on her forehead. "What was that for?" she asked. "I've just kissed the Blarney stone," he said. Needless to say, she got her price.

Kate with Cary Grant. (MOMA)

Kate was dating director George Stevens when she met Spencer Tracy on the set of Woman of the Year. (PHOTOFEST)

Spencer Tracy. (PHOTOFEST)

Kate had never met Spencer Tracy. But like most of her peers in Hollywood, she greatly admired his acting. Tracy was a difficult character—moody, unpredictable and alcoholic. But he was almost universally revered as an actor. Virtually everyone who worked with him—Clark Gable, Laurence Olivier, Elizabeth Taylor—would say that Tracy's acting was a revelation to them. His style was completely natural and unaffected; he simply became his part. Hit movies like *San Francisco*, *Boys' Town*, and *Captains Courageous* made him the king of the MGM lot.

Lucky for Kate (and for Tracy, too), his latest film, *The Yearling*, had run into snags during shooting on location in Florida. Unexpectedly, he was free. Mankiewicz sent him the script for *Woman of the Year*, and Tracy responded that he was interested.

Tracy liked Kate's acting, but he bristled at her public image, which struck him as a mixture of all that he loathed: intellectualism, aristocratic airs and, above all, pants. When Tracy first laid eyes on her holding court at the MGM canteen, her hands hidden in the pockets of her baggy trousers, he turned to Mankiewicz and said, "Not me, boy, I don't want to get mixed up with anything like that."

Mankiewicz, however, saw a spark of interest in Tracy's eyes. He invited Tracy to a private screening of *The Philadelphia Story*. And as the lights came up and he saw Tracy's face, he knew the actor was sold. "Damned fine actress," he said. Yes, he would sign on for *Woman of the Year*.

Two days later, the two were formally introduced on the MGM lot. Kate had just come from another heated negotiating session with Mayer. That morning, she had decked herself out for maximum impact. On her feet, she wore custom-made four-inch platform shoes that elevated her to nearly six feet in height. She wore them whenever she needed to feel formidable.

As Mankiewicz introduced Kate to her new co-star, Kate stood up, towering over Tracy's five-nine frame. She smiled as they shook hands. "I'm afraid I'm a little tall for you, Mr. Tracy," she said.

Tracy glared up into her eyes. "Don't worry, Miss Hepburn," he said. "I'll cut you down to my size." They both laughed and said goodbye, feeling confident that their collaboration would be a successful one. And indeed it would be, in ways that neither one could have hoped or expected.

CHAPTER SEVEN

"Living was never easy for Spence."

SPENCER TRACY WAS BORN in 1900, in Milwaukee, Wisconsin. His mother, Carrie, was a New England Protestant. His father, John, was a Catholic who instilled a deep sense of religion in his son.

Tracy was an indifferent student who spent more time getting in brawls than he did on serious academics. High school was a patchwork of Catholic schools from which he was continually thrown out. Somehow he graduated and was accepted at Ripon College. It was there that he developed his taste for drama. Very quickly, people noticed that he possessed some impressive gifts, not the least of which was his ability to memorize a script after one read-through.

Tracy eventually moved to New York, where he was hired by a respectable Westchester stock company. He met his wife there, a pretty brunette actress named Louise Treadwell. They married on September 13, 1923, and soon had their first child. Their son, John, was born deaf. Tracy adored his son, but was never able to come to terms with his condition; he would always believe that he was somehow responsible for his son's disability.

Before long, Tracy was in Hollywood, playing mainly convicts and gangsters in forgettable films. His role in *The Power and the Glory*, written by Preston Sturges, was a turning point; critics raved. "Spencer Tracy's railroad president is one of the fullest characterizations ever achieved on the screen." Audiences, however, were slower to recognize his talents. And his studio, Fox, grew tired of behavior that was often uncooperative and erratic. When Fox didn't renew his contract, MGM snapped him up.

Louis B. Mayer made it his mission to find vehicles that would showcase Tracy's great gifts; his craggy looks made him an unlikely candidate for a traditional romantic leading man, but Mayer felt that there was more for Tracy than criminals and bums. He hit pay dirt with *Fury*, directed by Fritz Lang, which was another critical success, and *San Francisco*, which was both a critical and box-office smash.

Tracy with his daughter, Susie, in 1939. (PHOTOFEST)

With *San Francisco*, Tracy became MGM's biggest money-maker and one of Hollywood's most popular leading men. But success did not tame the demons that had been tormenting Tracy for much of his life. His blunt and anti-intellectual persona masked a character of great complexity, one that contained both flashes of artistic brilliance and a capacity for crippling despair. "Living was never easy for Spence," Kate told Christopher Anderson. "He was deeply troubled, not at all like that totally confident figure the public saw up there on the screen. But whatever it was that made him so unhappy, he never talked about it—not with me, not to anyone. I realize now that I never really knew him."

By the late 1930s, Tracy's reputation as an actor was rivaled by his reputation as a drinker and a womanizer, two passions, friends say, that helped Tracy manage his bouts of depression. He never appeared drunk on a set. But he would disappear for days at a time during his drinking binges, often causing chaos on the set of whatever film he happened to be shooting at the time.

His marriage to Louise crumbled under the strain of several of Tracy's highly publicized affairs, most notably with Loretta Young, whom he met in 1933 on the set of their film, *A Man's Castle*. Tracy made no attempt to hide his romance with this beautiful starlet, who was just nineteen years old when they met. The couple was photographed together all over Hollywood.

But Tracy had always sworn that he would never get divorced. To Tracy, his Catholic vows of marriage were sacred. In 1934, Loretta Young issued this statement: "Since Spence and I are both Catholic and can never be married, we have agreed not to see each other again."

Tracy returned to Louise, but their marriage never recovered. Tracy spent many nights in a hotel room he rented in Beverly Hills. Louise was completely absorbed with her work as a pioneer for education for deaf children, a crusade that won her respect throughout Hollywood. They separated for good in 1938, though Tracy would remain closely involved with his two children and with Louise, whom he would always support in high style.

Nothing in Kate's romantic history would have suggested that she would devote herself to someone like Spencer Tracy. Her three most serious relationships—with Luddy, Leland Hayward, and Howard Hughes—were with men who mainly offered her good companionship. She had never taken on such a complex character, and never opened herself up to a relationship like the one she so admired in her parents.

She was thirty-three when she met Tracy, and she seemed to have accepted that her life would not include that kind of everlasting love. There would be "beaux" and close friends. And of course there would be her family. But she did not imagine more.

Sparks flew on the set of Woman of the Year. (BEN CARBONETTO)

From Woman of the Year, *1942.*
(MOMA)

Into this mind-set walked Spencer Tracy. In virtually every respect, the two were opposites. Tracy acted on instinct, never rehearsed, and generally gave his best performances on the first take.
Kate loved to labor over a script, to research her roles and to refine her
performance through a laborious cycle of rehearsal, discussion and
more rehearsal. Tracy was a Catholic whose religion shaped his life
and tortured his conscience. Kate was a non-believer whose only real
"religion" was self-reliance.

Still, within a few days on the set of *Woman of the Year*, it was clear
to them (and everyone on the set) that a serious romance was in store.
George Stevens, among the first to notice, gallantly stepped aside.

Over the next thirty years, Kate would nourish and support Tracy.
She accepted that they would never marry—it never bothered her.
And she encouraged him to spend time with his children. His drinking
problem didn't disappear, but he binged less often, and years would
go by when he didn't drink at all.

Woman of the Year, which critics liked and audiences adored, established Tracy and Hepburn as one of the great on-screen duos. "We balanced out each other's natures," Kate once said. "We were the perfect representation of the American male and female. The woman is always pretty sharp, and she's needling the man, sort of like a mosquito. The man is always slowly coming along, and she needles, and then he slowly puts out his big paw and slaps the lady down, and that's attractive to the American public. He's the ultimate boss of the situation, and he's very challenged by her. It isn't an easy kingdom for him to maintain. That—in simple terms—is what he did."

In pairing her up with Tracy—a "man's man"—Hollywood had discovered a way to mediate Kate's strong personality. Even at the height of her popularity, Kate was never able to capture the heart of middle America. Her fans came from older, more educated and sophisticated quarters. Tracy, on the other hand, had widespread appeal.

(BEN CARBONETTO)

In many of their films (and most potently in *Woman of the Year*), Kate's independent character was always chastened by her devotion to her leading man. If Kate minded this rather anti-feminist slant to many of her films, she never said so. Neither did she mind that Tracy always got top billing in the films they did together. When Garson Kanin once wondered out loud whether Tracy thought that such an arrangement was a tad unchivalrous, Tracy responded, "This is a movie, chowderhead, not a lifeboat."

Between 1942 and 1967, Tracy and Hepburn did nine films together. They followed *Woman of the Year* with *Keeper of the Flame*, a turgid story with a cautionary message about the spread of Fascism in America. Kate and Tracy shared strong liberal views, and were eager to do a "message" film. But the story lacked the two components that would prove central to the success of the Hepburn/Tracy team—love and comedy.

Kate played Christine Forrest, the wife of Robert V. Forrest, an American icon who is as famous for his patriotism as he is for his business empire (the character was based on Louis B. Mayer's friend William Randolph Hearst). Tracy played Steven O'Malley, a newspaper reporter who uncovers the fact that Forrest's jingoism was a front for Fascist activities.

The film had promise. But the story had some glitches that Donald Ogden Stewart wasn't able to iron out of his script. George Cukor, who directed, struggled to breathe some life into it. But in the end, as he said, the whole affair looked like it took place in a "wax museum."

Before beginning filming on *Keeper of the Flame*, Kate had traveled East to appear in a new Philip Barry play, *Without Love*. She had hoped to take the play to Broadway. But problems with the script and a complete lack of chemistry between Kate and her rather soggy leading man, Elliott Nugent, stalled the play on the road. She was delighted to get back to Hollywood and her life with Tracy.

Despite the failure of *Without Love* on the stage, Louis B. Mayer bought the film rights for Tracy and Hepburn, whom he now viewed as his most bankable team. Donald Ogden Stewart fleshed out Tracy's part and succeeded in creating an appealing comedy about a slow-burning love affair between a widow and an inventor. *Without Love* isn't the strongest of the Tracy/Hepburn comedies, but it was a hit for the studio and it put the team back on course.

By this time, Kate and Tracy were spending virtually all of their

Kate and Tracy in Keeper of the Flame. (MOMA)

Kate on stage in Without Love, *1942.* (PHOTOFEST)

(ABOVE RIGHT)
Kate with Elliott Nugent in the stage version of Without Love.
(BEN CARBONETTO)

(RIGHT)
Kate and Tracy in the screen version of Without Love, *1945.*
(MOMA)

Without Love. (MOMA)

time together. Spencer returned home many weekends to be with his children, John and Susie. But the rest of the time he was with Kate, either at her home or at the cottage he rented on the grounds of George Cukor's estate.

Tracy never ventured onto a golf course and Kate never even tried to get him to pick up a tennis racket. But she was able to introduce him to some of her passions, particularly the outdoors. They both enjoyed painting landscapes and taking long walks. Overall, Kate succeeded in distracting him from the dark moods that periodically descended on him. And she usually managed to keep him out of the company of his gang of drinking buddies, which included Jimmy Cagney, Clark Gable, Victor Fleming, and Pat O'Brien.

One of the books that Kate and Tracy had discovered together was *The Sea of Grass*, a Western saga about a man's complicated love affair with both his land and his wife. They urged Mayer to buy the rights

LOUISE TREADWELL TRACY

Spencer Tracy and Louise Treadwell were both struggling actors working at a Westchester stock theater company when they met and fell in love. Louise was four years older than Tracy and the more experienced actor; she had played some small roles on Broadway.

Her colleagues regarded her as a solid actress, and she hoped to continue even after she and Tracy were married. But when their first child, John, was born profoundly deaf, she devoted herself to what she saw as her real calling: caring for her son and pioneering the field of education for deaf children.

Spencer's career took off after they moved to Hollywood, and they had their second child, Susie. But Spencer's appetite for other women strained their marriage. They split for good in the late thirties, although they would never divorce. Gossip held that Louise wouldn't let Tracy go. In fact it was Spencer—the devout Catholic—who refused to submit to a divorce. Louise herself was an Episcopalian.

By the time they split, Louise was consumed with her crusade to help deaf children and their parents. In 1942, she founded the John Tracy Clinic to help other parents with deaf children. The clinic quickly outgrew its small quarters on the University of Southern California campus. Aggressive fund-raising (fueled by stars borrowed from MGM) helped Louise park the clinic in a spacious new building.

Her efforts earned an international reputation for the John Tracy Clinic and tremendous respect for Louise within Hollywood. She was so highly

Louise and Spencer Tracy out on the town. (PHOTOFEST)

for their next vehicle, and convinced Elia Kazan to sign on as director. Kazan's success with *A Tree Grows in Brooklyn* the year before had made him a hot property.

From the outset, Kazan sensed a disaster in the making. He found it difficult to penetrate the private world that Kate and Tracy shared together. And both of their performances suffered from the lack of a strong directorial hand. Kate's Lutie Cameron, a frustrated wife, seemed "patronizing" to one critic and "as pert as a sparrow" to another. Tracy, who played her husband, Colonel James Brewton, was so staid that he was often lost in the breathtaking scenery. Both Kate and Tracy consider *The Sea of Grass* to be the low-point of their career together.

While both Kate and Spencer made it a priority to find films they could work on together, each continued to pursue their solo careers. Neither had much success. Following *Woman of the Year*, in fact, Kate found herself in a slump reminiscent of her *Mary of Scotland* and *Quality Street* days. In good times and bad, Mayer valued Kate's presence on his lot; she was his prestige star and he adored her. But his studio did little to help her find the right vehicles.

Aside from her work with Tracy, she appeared in three films between 1944 and 1947: *Dragon Seed*, *Undercurrent*, and *Song of Love*; all were critical and financial disappointments.

Dragon Seed, based on a novel by Pearl S. Buck, focused on life in Japanese-occupied China and the hardships and atrocities that were making headlines in America. Kate played Jade, a Chinese peasant woman with an independent streak. MGM's makeup department transformed Kate into a serviceable Asian woman (her cheekbones certainly helped matters). And as in *Keeper of the Flame*, Kate relished the chance to play in a picture that contained a substantive message.

Undercurrent was Kate's only classic thriller. It was another flop, but it did spark a friendship between Kate and Judy Garland, who was married to *Undercurrent*'s director, Vincente Minnelli. Kate took a maternal interest in Garland, who, like Spencer Tracy, was often crippled by periods of depression. Kate did her best to encourage Garland to focus more attention on her physical health, and hooked Garland into her own vast network of doctors (handpicked by

regarded in Hollywood that even the gossip reporters wanted to protect her. Although Tracy's affair with Kate was well known throughout the movie industry, the Hollywood magazines never breathed a word to the public. No one wanted to offend Louise Tracy.

Kate as Lutie Cameron and Tracy as Colonel James Brewton in The Sea of Grass, *1947.* (MOMA)

Kate and Turhan Bey in Dragon Seed, *1944.* (MOMA)

(BELOW RIGHT)
Kate with Robert Taylor in Undercurrent, *1946.* (PHOTOFEST)

Kate as Jade. (PHOTOFEST)

Kate as Clara Schumann in Song of Love, *1947.* (PHOTOFEST)

Kate with Robert Walker in Song of Love. (PHOTOFEST)

Dr. Hepburn himself). In later years, as Garland became more tangled in her addictions and depressions, Kate remained a loyal friend.

In 1948, with four failures in her wake, Kate was brought back from the brink of a serious career crisis by a last-minute opportunity to star opposite Tracy in *State of the Union*. Claudette Colbert had been set to co-star in this political drama. But days before shooting, she ripped up her contract when director Frank Capra refused to submit to her increasingly outlandish scheduling demands.

With thousands of dollars already sunk in pre-production and a whole crew standing by to begin filming, MGM and Capra were in a panic.

As it happened, Kate was familiar with the script, which had been lying around Tracy's house for weeks. When Capra called Tracy to tell him of the Colbert fiasco, Tracy remained calm. He knew just the woman for the job. The next day, Saturday, Kate was with the costume designer being fitted in Colbert's costumes. That Monday, she was on the set to begin shooting.

State of the Union is the story of an idealistic politician and the people who try to lead him astray. Kate played the wife who stands by helplessly watching her husband being corrupted and who in the end leads him back onto the right path.

In 1948, with the House Un-American Activities Committee turning its attention toward Hollywood, this kind of political—and overtly liberal-leaning—picture was considered controversial and risky for those involved. The atmosphere on the set was tense; Adolphe Menjou, one of the stars, was an outspoken conservative who was openly contemptuous of Kate's more liberal perspective and her passionate support of Henry Wallace, Roosevelt's former vice-president and the third-party candidate opposing Truman.

Both Kate and Tracy loathed Menjou for naming names at a HUAC probe into "Communist sympathizers" allegedly trying to corrupt America through the movies. The year before, Kate had taken the podium at an anti-censorship rally where she had condemned the HUAC investigations. "Scratch a do-gooder like Hepburn," Menjou once said, "and they'll yell Pravda."

"Scratch a Hepburn," Tracy responded, "and you'll get kicked in

State of the Union, *1948*. (MOMA)

State of the Union. (MOMA)

Kate, Tracy, Angela Lansbury and Van Johnson in State of the Union. (PHOTOFEST)

the ass." Tracy himself, despite his strong liberal bent, preferred to remain aloof from politics. Acting and politics, he believed, was a dangerous mix. "Remember who shot Lincoln," he often said, only half-joking.

Despite the tensions on the set of *State of the Union* (or perhaps because of them), Kate gave one of her best performances in years. The film wasn't terribly successful, but critics praised it, and Kate's confidence surged. She also won the admiration of yet another top director: Frank Capra. "There are women and there are women and then there is Katie," he said. "There are actresses and there are actresses and then there is Hepburn. A rare professional-amateur, acting is her hobby and her living and her love. She is wedded to her vocation as a nun is to hers, and as competitive in acting as Sonja Henie was in ice-skating. No clock-watching, no humbug, no sham temperament. If she made up her mind to become a runner, she'd be the first woman to break the four-minute mile."

Although Kate and Tracy never ventured out in public, they did socialize with a small circle of friends that included George Cukor, Jane Loring, Laura Harding (whom Tracy merely tolerated), scenarist R. L. Jones, producer Chester Erskine, and Garson Kanin and Ruth Gordon, a married team of writers.

Kate with Frank Capra on the set of State of the Union. (PHOTOFEST)

State of the Union. (MOMA)

Gordon and Kanin had been anxious to come up with an idea worthy of their friends. They finally succeeded with *Adam's Rib*, the story of a pair of married lawyers who take opposite sides in a tumultuous legal case.

Adam's Rib showed off Kate and Tracy as a loving and devoted couple: Adam and Amanda Bonner, whose lavish social life and demanding careers never distract them from their top priority: each other. Trouble strikes when Amanda decides to defend a blonde bombshell (Judy Holliday) who killed her husband in a fit of jealousy over his blatant womanizing. Adam Bonner happens to be the attorney prosecuting the state's case against the woman. The result is a classic war-between-the-sexes comedy intertwined with some rather lofty notions of sexism and equality. In one impassioned speech,

Adam's Rib, *1949.* (PHOTOFEST)

Kate's Amanda echoes the views broadcast by Kit Hepburn during her various crusades for women's rights.

The film is occasionally stagey and slick. But it was a hit—critically and financially. "Mr. Tracy and Miss Hepburn are the stellar performances in the show and their perfect compatibility in comic capers is delightful to see," wrote Bosley Crowther in *The New York Times*. "A line thrown away, a lifted eyebrow, a smile, or a sharp, resounding slap on a tender part of the anatomy is as natural as breathing to them . . . Miss Holliday is simply hilarious as a dumb but stubborn dame." Both director George Cukor and Kate had worked to ensure that Holliday be given every chance to win over audiences, and their efforts paid off. *Adam's Rib* launched her as a major star.

Adam's Rib. (PHOTOFEST)

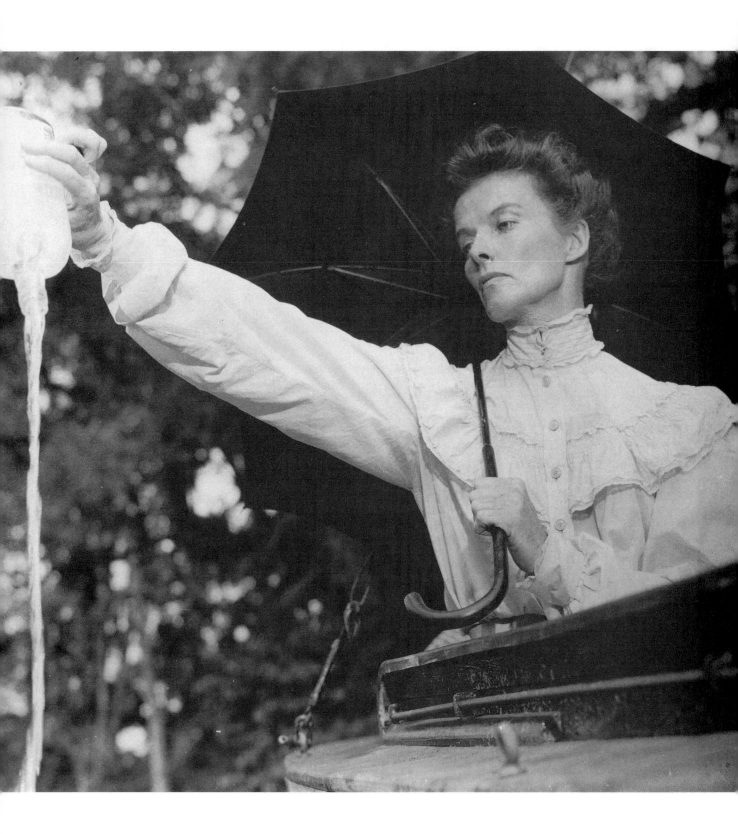

CHAPTER EIGHT

"What there is, is 'cherce.'"

Kate as Rose Sayer in
The African Queen.
(BEN CARBONETTO)

A S KATE'S HOLLYWOOD CAREER sailed along with unusual ease, her family life suffered its first crisis since Tom's death decades before.

In March 1951, Kate was visiting her parents in Hartford when her mother suddenly died. Kate and her father had taken a day-trip to Fenwick. When they returned to Hartford in time for five o'clock tea, they found the tea table set, but the house was strangely quiet. Looking at each other, they raced upstairs, where they found Kit lying across her bed. Kate took her hand, which was still warm.

As with Tom's death nearly thirty years before, the family banded together for strength. And then they moved forward. Before the year was out, Dr. Hepburn was remarried to one of his nurses, Madeline Santa Croce. Dr. Hepburn's decision to sell the Hartford house was a blow to all of the kids. But Kate and the others believed they should support anything he needed to do to get over the loss of Kit.

Following Kit's funeral, Kate dove headlong into her next project: *The African Queen.* It would prove to be one of the most arduous experiences of her life, and perhaps the greatest performance of her career.

Director John Huston brought Kate, Humphrey Bogart, and a cast and crew of nearly fifty people deep into British Uganda. In addition to whatever disasters routinely plague an elaborate film shoot, the cast and crew of *The African Queen* confronted scorching temperatures, soaking humidity, deadly poisonous snakes, stinging ants, and debilitating illnesses.

For Kate, the role of Rosie Sayer was a supreme challenge. Never before had she played someone with fewer affects, a woman whose substance lay deep beneath a meek and stern surface. Nor had she ever appeared on film without makeup, with her freckles and forty-four years' worth of crow's-feet proudly on display.

Rosie has spent her adult life serving God and her brother in a remote mission in German East Africa. World War I has just begun, and German troops are rampaging through Africa. When they strike Rose's village, burning it to the ground, her brother, Samuel, is so distraught that he dies. Rosie is left alone.

Enter Charlie Allnut, a sweet drunk who earns his living running errands in his riverboat, *The African Queen*. He rescues Rose from the ruins of her village and suggests that the two wait out the war in the quiet of the marshy river. Freed from the confines of her ordered life, Rosie feels galvanized. She convinces Charlie that they should take action against the Germans. They decide to make the dangerous journey down the wild river to sink the German gunboat patrolling the area. In the process, the unlikely pair fall in love.

Poisoned by contaminated water (which Huston and Bogart shunned in favor of whiskey), Kate lost nearly twenty pounds from her lean frame. Shooting was constantly disrupted by illness and problems, and during the final stages, the whole production was forced to leave Africa to finish up on a set in England.

But to Kate, the experience was well worth the pain and suffering. Both she and Bogart were nominated for Academy Awards, and she was proud to have forged a relationship with John Huston. Years later, Huston admitted he had seriously fallen for Kate. But, he said, "she was a one-man woman. There was never anyone but Tracy." In 1987, Kate wrote a bestselling book about the ordeal: *The Making of "The African Queen" Or How I Went to Africa with Bogart, Bacall and Huston and Almost Lost My Mind*.

Kate returned to the US with a trunk full of souvenirs and a new lease on her career. In playing Rosie, Kate knew that she had stepped

Kate with John Huston during the arduous filming of The African Queen, *1951.* (BEN CARBONETTO)

Kate with John Huston. (MOMA)

squarely into middle age. Many actors suffer this transition. But Kate sensed that she was beginning a new and more comfortable chapter in her life.

She and Tracy settled back in Hollywood to undertake their next film together: another Kanin/Gordon creation, *Pat and Mike*. The story revolved around the relationship between Kate's Pat Pemberton, a physical education teacher and all-around star athlete, and Mike Conovan, a sports promoter who wants to make Pat a star and himself some big bucks. Gordon and Kanin wanted to give Kate a chance to showcase her tremendous athletic skills, and even Cukor, her lifelong friend, was shocked to see her gifts in action. After nearly wasting away on the set of *The African Queen*, Kate was pleased to be able to get back into shape.

Kate, Humphrey Bogart and Lauren Bacall return from Africa in July 1951. (BETTMANN ARCHIVE)

Pat and Mike. (PHOTOFEST)

The film worked well enough. There was the requisite amount of tension between well-bred Pat and rough-hewn Mike and plenty of snappy dialogue. In fact, it yielded one of the great Hepburn/Tracy lines: referring to Pat's toned body, Mike says in his Brooklyn accent, "There's not much meat on her, but what there is, is cherce."

Pat and Mike was Kate's last film at MGM. Louis B. Mayer had been replaced by Dore Schary, who was not terribly eager to indulge Mayer's old stable of luminaries. The studio system was officially dead. And in any case, Kate was eager to branch out in different directions. She decided to venture out on her own.

Her first stop was London, where she performed in a stage production of George Bernard Shaw's *The Millionairess*. The Brits loved it. Kate was compelled to take the show to Broadway, where she performed in a ten-week limited engagement. It wasn't her long-awaited Broadway triumph. But reviewers were kind and the run was sold out from end-to-end.

Summertime followed, a David Lean production filmed in Venice. The film, about yet another spinster who finds unlikely love in a far-off land, was moderately successful. But it was not worth the price; the script called for Kate to take a spill into the filthy Venetian canals. Despite precautions—disinfectant dumped in the area into which Kate would fall, ointments protecting her entire body—Kate ended up with a serious case of conjunctivitis. It turned out to be incurable, and has left Kate with the moist-eyed expression she's worn ever since.

When Kate finally returned to Hollywood, she and Tracy had been separated for the better part of a year. Tracy had not fared well in Kate's absence. Without her stabilizing influence, he had sunk into his drinking routine. He was massively depressed and feeling the pains of his alcohol-ravaged body. His drinking and irrational behavior had gotten him fired from his last picture, *Tribute to a Bad Man*. The inside buzz was that Tracy's career was finished.

For nearly fourteen years, Kate had been tending to Tracy's

On stage with Robert Helpmann in The Millionairess. (PHOTOFEST)

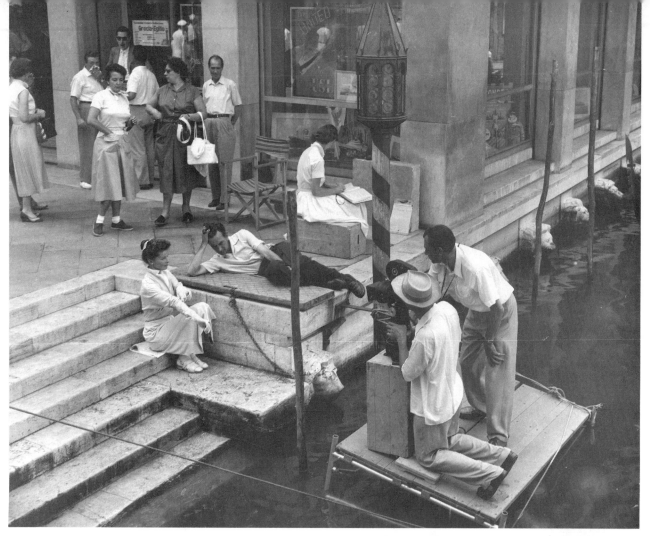

In Venice with director David Lean, shooting
Summertime, *1955.* (BEN CARBONETTO)   (MOMA)

With David Lean. (BEN CARBONETTO)

household, supervising most of his meals, orchestrating his social life, and helping him maintain his uneasy equilibrium. But she had clearly underestimated the level of his dependence on her. Never again, she resolved, would she allow herself to be separated from him for such a protracted period. She made good on her commitment to appear as a Russian airwoman in the film *The Iron Petticoat*. But once that was completed, she devoted herself completely to Tracy—to resuscitating his career, to restoring his confidence, and to helping him maintain what was left of his health. Without Kate, most of Tracy's friends believed, he surely would have died a lonely and miserable death.

Over the next decade, Kate retreated almost entirely from her career. She appeared in just two films without Tracy, and neither was worth her energies.

As Russian Airforce Captain Vinka Kovelenko in The Iron Petticoat, *1956.* (PHOTOFEST)

With Burt Lancaster in The Rainmaker, *1956.* (PHOTOFEST)

Kate and Tracy in Desk Set, *1957.* (PHOTOFEST)

Suddenly, Last Summer, released in 1959, was an overwrought and homophobic story of a woman (Kate) bent on hiding her family's sordid history from the public. "I loathe this film," wrote C. A. Lejeune of *The Observer*. "To my mind, it is a decadent piece of work, sensational, barbarous, and ridiculous." Kate, as she would later admit, agreed with Lejeune's (and most critics') assessment.

Long Day's Journey Into Night, the film version of Eugene O'Neill's play, was a more noble effort. But Kate was miscast as Mary Tyrone, a woman who is addicted to morphine she was first given to cope with complications that accompanied the birth of her son. Critics admired the film, especially Sidney Lumet's direction. But it was not a success.

Meanwhile, with Kate's support, Tracy's career rebounded. "She was spending all her time looking after Spence," director Stanley Kramer told writer Bill Davidson. "She would arrive with him in the morning, making sure he took his medicines and drank his milk, leaving with him when he was through in the afternoon. She was like a nurse-companion to him, or a wife."

Hit films like *Judgment at Nuremburg, Inherit the Wind* and even the cult favorite *It's a Mad Mad Mad Mad World* elevated Tracy to a new level of stardom. Critics who just a few years before had urged Tracy to retire were sainting him as a living legend.

Kate claimed that her time with Tracy, under any circumstances, was precious to her, well worth any movie role she might have passed up. Still, dealing with Tracy wasn't easy. Friends like the Kanins often cringed at the cutting remarks he habitually lobbed her way. He called her "the bag of bones," and often condemned what he viewed as her intellectual airs. But as Kate has said, that was simply his style. She never doubted that he loved her, and she never regretted a moment of their time together.

A Long Day's Journey into Night, *1962.* (MOMA)

"... mine must be for the both of us."

BETWEEN 1963 AND 1966, Tracy's health was so fragile that neither he nor Kate worked at all. His kidneys were failing. His liver was barely functioning. He was so prone to respiratory problems that he had an oxygen tank in his bedroom at home.

Stanley Kramer, a director and close friend of Tracy's, had made it his mission to find a project that would lure Tracy back to the screen—perhaps, he suspected, for the last time.

Guess Who's Coming to Dinner proved to be irresistible to both Tracy and Kate. Written by William Rose, the story dealt with an interracial marriage and its impact on the families of the bride and groom.

Kate and Tracy played Matt and Christina Drayton, a pair of wealthy San Franciscans whose identities as freethinkers are tested when their daughter, Joey, announces that she is planning to marry John Prentice, a black man. For the role of Prentice, Kramer hired Sidney Poitier, who Kramer believed projected the high level of nobility and achievement required for Americans of 1967 to accept the notion of interracial marriage. Poitier's character was not only a

Guess Who's Coming to Dinner,
1967. (PHOTOFEST)

*Katharine Houghton and Sidney
Poitier in* Guess Who's Coming to
Dinner. (PHOTOFEST)

With niece Katharine Houghton in
Guess Who's Coming to Dinner.

On the set of Guess Who's Coming
to Dinner. (MOMA)

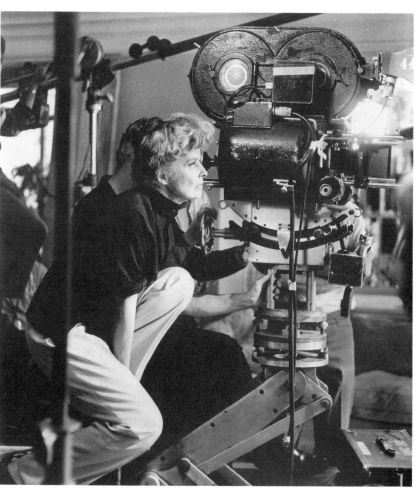

doctor, but he held a prestigious position with World Health Organization. For good measure, writer Rose threw in a Nobel Prize nomination.

Kramer didn't have an actress in mind for the role of Joey Drayton. And when Kate suggested her niece for the role, Kramer allowed himself to be convinced. Katharine Houghton had the right look—beautiful and aristocratic (a ringer for her aunt). Besides, with Kate, Tracy and Poitier anchoring the cast, he could afford to take a chance on a newcomer.

Everyone was excited to be working on a ground-breaking film, even with its absurd padding of Poitier's character. But the mood on the set was delicate. Kramer faced a great challenge in trying to work around Tracy's frail health. The actor could work for only four hours a day. Kramer hired a double to stand in for Tracy's non-speaking shots. Kate was constantly hovering around, trying to make sure Tracy wasn't overexerting himself. Still, shooting finished on time, and those on the set remember that last day as extremely emotional; tears flowed all around, even from Tracy's eyes.

Released in 1967, *Guess Who's Coming to Dinner* was an enormous hit, the biggest of Kate's career. Most critics felt that Kramer and Rose's conception of race relations in America was laughably simplistic. But even the most vicious critics were taken with Tracy's performance, and Kate's, too. Both were nominated for Academy Awards.

Tracy didn't survive to read his reviews or to hear about his nomination. He died just twelve days after shooting finished. Kate found him at three A.M. sitting at his kitchen table. He was sixty-seven years old.

Kate had just a few minutes alone with him before his brother Carroll arrived with Louise, John and Susie. She did not attend the funeral. That, she believed, was for Louise and the children.

Months later, Kate was in France filming *The Lion in Winter* when she received a phone call informing her that she had won the Oscar for Best Actress for her performance in *Guess Who's Coming to Dinner*. She immediately asked if Tracy had won, too. He hadn't. "Well," Kate said, "mine must be for the both of us."

Tracy's death transformed Kate's life. She had lost the only man whom she ever honestly loved, someone who had given her life both shape and meaning for twenty-five years.

But it also freed her. As Kate has said, the life she shared with Tracy was built around his habits—the foods he liked to eat, the people he enjoyed seeing, the places he wanted to visit, and in the last years especially, the limitations imposed by his frail health. Now it was time for Kate to create a life that was all hers.

It soon became clear that the primary setting for this new life would be the East Coast. She took over Tracy's cottage as her California residence. But for the past twenty-five years, Kate has spent most of her time in New York City and Fenwick. In New York she gardens in her backyard, goes to the theater whenever she can, and encourages friends to dine with her at her town house (she is a fine cook who is particularly famous for her brownies).

At Fenwick she still swims whenever she can, although she no longer does one-and-a-halfs off the pier. In the spring and summer, she spends most of her time in the garden. "My hands are strong—I can sift and get out the old crab-grass roots and dump in the topsoil and humus and peat and manure and mix them with sand," she says. "I can still crawl through the flower beds."

Both of her houses are cluttered with artifacts from all phases of her life. "There is no design," she says of both houses. "They are not decorated, there are no curtains, everything is casual." In the reading room of the town house, a carved wooden goose hovers over Kate's favorite reading chair, a treasure from Tracy's cottage. Her own landscape paintings—usually of bunches of flowers or of the sea— lean against most available walls. Her bed is adorned with a small needlepoint pillow inscribed with the words, "Listen to the Song of Life." These were the words carved into the fireplace at the Hepburn family home in Hartford.

Many in Hollywood expected Kate to retire completely after Tracy's death, to recede gracefully and allow the black-and-white images of her glamour days to stand for her whole life.

Not only did she continue to work, but she forged an entirely new relationship with American moviegoers. Her performance in *Guess Who's Coming to Dinner* seemed to melt the ambivalence that so many had viewed her with. She became nothing short of an institution. For the first time in her career, Kate began to feel that audiences and the press were actually "rooting for her."

Kate's attitude about her privacy hasn't softened. But her feelings about the press have. She has slowly opened her life to both the press and the public. And in 1983, when Louise Tracy died, Kate even started to talk about her relationship with Tracy—"her great and good friend." In 1986, she organized a televised tribute to Tracy, aided by her close friend, Susie Tracy, Spencer's daughter.

She has worked steadily over the past twenty-five years, looking for roles that are "fascinating." She has scored some major hits. Just a year after Tracy's death, she starred in *The Lion in Winter*, a rather tragic comedy about Eleanor of Aquitaine, Henry II and their highly dysfunctional family. Kate was excited to work with Peter O'Toole, who had been cast as Henry. And both Kate and O'Toole clicked instantly with director Anthony Harvey. "A passion for life, that thing about Katharine Hepburn," Harvey said. "She adores every moment. She is always amazed."

Critics were unanimous in their assessment of Kate's performance. "Miss Hepburn is virtually faultless, with an irrepressible elegance and charm making her thoroughly believable both as a queen and a woman," wrote Thomas Brennan of *The Villager*. Kate was nominated for yet another Academy Award, bringing her total number of nominations up to eleven, a record. No one imagined that she'd win two years in a row. But she did win—tying with Barbra Streisand—to bring home her third Oscar in the Best Actress category. Kate has said that next to Jo March in *Little Women*, Eleanor is her favorite of all the dozens of characters she has played in her career.

As Eleanor of Aquitaine in The Lion in Winter. (PHOTOFEST)

With Peter O'Toole in The Lion in Winter, *1968.* (MOMA)

PLAYBILL

the national magazine for theatregoers

COCO

(PHOTOFEST)

As Coco Chanel on Broadway in 1969. (PHOTOFEST)

As Queen Hecuba in The Trojan Women, *1971.* (MOMA)

Seven years later, Kate scored another major box-office hit with *Rooster Cogburn*, which teamed her up with John Wayne. The film, a sequel to Wayne's 1969 hit, *True Grit*, was in many ways a classic Western—an old gunslinger on his last crusade. But it was also a love story. Kate played Eula Goodnight, an uptight New Englander who pairs up with Rooster Cogburn to pursue the band of outlaws that killed her father. Like Rosie and Charlie in *The African Queen*, Eula and Marshall Cogburn are bound together by their adventure and wind up falling in love.

Many in Hollywood were shocked to hear that Kate, an avowed liberal, was looking forward to working with Wayne, a virulent conservative who had headed up the Motion Picture Alliance for the Preservation of American Ideals, an organization that helped blacklist so many in Hollywood during the 1950s. But despite their political differences, the two felt an instant kinship with each other. And their obvious affection for each other had everything to do with the success of the film. "She's so feminine—she's a man's woman," Wayne said of Kate. "Imagine how she must have been at age twenty-five or thirty . . . how lucky a man would have been to have found her." Kate was equally admiring of Wayne. "What an experience," she said of working with him. "He's one hell of an actor."

In Rooster Cogburn, *1975.* (MOMA)

With John Wayne in Rooster Cogburn. (MOMA)

The film that would come to symbolize the latter phase of Kate's career was not the flamboyant *The Lion in Winter* or the appealing *Rooster Cogburn*. It was a simple and sentimental family drama: *On Golden Pond*. The film teamed her up with Henry Fonda. Kate had worked with just about all of the old-time male stars: John Barrymore, Cary Grant, Jimmy Stewart, Humphrey Bogart, John Wayne and Spencer Tracy. But she had never worked with Fonda. She wasn't even sure that they had met.

With Laurence Olivier in the TV movie, Love Among the Ruins, *1975.* (PHOTOFEST)

On the set of Love Among the Ruins. (ACADEMY OF MOTION PICTURE ARTS AND SCIENCES)

The film was based on a Broadway play that had disappeared rather quickly. But Kate saw it, and imagined herself in the role of Ethel Thayer, a woman who tries to bridge the emotional gap between her husband and her grown daughter. Jane Fonda had also seen the play, and was convinced that her father was made for the role of Ethel's husband, Norman. Fonda wanted to play the Thayers' daughter, Chelsea, herself. Henry and Jane Fonda had first-hand experience with troubled father/daughter relationships.

The film would later be credited with reestablishing the validity of mature films in post–*Star Wars* Hollywood. But it faced several major obstacles and nearly wasn't produced.

Despite the combined track records of Kate, Henry Fonda and Jane Fonda, there weren't many studios eager to bankroll a movie that revolved around a fifty-odd-year-old romance between two married people. Jane Fonda had to produce the film herself through her personal production company.

Once filming was set, Kate seriously injured her shoulder during a routine tennis game, and had to have emergency surgery. With shooting set to begin in just weeks, Kate's doctors were urging her to put aside at least four months to recover. Naturally, Kate refused, convinced that she could accelerate her recovery through her own methods. And she did.

There was also the problem of a threatened strike by the Screen Actors Guild, which delayed the production of dozens of films. But with Henry Fonda in frail health and Jane Fonda committed to a full slate of future projects, delaying *On Golden Pond* would mean canceling it. Jane Fonda was able to work around the strike by negotiating her own deal with SAG.

Kate could not have been more at home on Big Squam Lake, where *On Golden Pond* was shot. She stayed in a rambling house (the best on the lot) and despite lingering pain in her shoulder, she swam every day, morning and evening. She was the first to arrive on the set, and greeted Henry Fonda and his wife, Shirlee, with a small dinner party at which she presented Fonda with a gift: one of Tracy's old hats.

As she had in *Guess Who's Coming to Dinner*, Kate subdued her role,

In the TV movie, The Corn Is Green, *1979.* (PHOTOFEST)

With Henry Fonda in On Golden Pond, *1981.* (PHOTOFEST)

LAUREN TARSHIS

never wanting to outshine her male co-star. This was Henry Fonda's film, she believed (and it would be his last). Her Ethel Thayer is among her most appealing roles, and it's easy to see why audiences fell in love with her.

The film, produced for under $8 million, was an enormous success, earning ten Oscar nominations, including Best Picture, Best Actress (Kate) and Best Actor (Henry Fonda). Few were surprised when Henry Fonda won for Best Actor. But Kate's win—her fourth—shocked the house.

Although Kate has said that "growing old is no fun at all," she has become a virtual symbol of doing it gracefully. Her regimen of exercise has kept her body strong, although at times she has had to struggle to keep it in one piece. Still, after one hip replacement, a car accident that nearly cost her a foot, and operations on her shoulder and eyes, she's remarkably fit.

She has continued to work, completing four films since *On Golden Pond*: *The Ultimate Solution of Grace Quigley*, *Mrs. Delafield Wants to Marry*, *Laura Lansing Slept Here* and the TV movie *The Man Upstairs*. She continues the pursuit—of opportunities, of pleasure, of perfection—that motivated her as a young woman and keeps her vital today.

"We're surrounded by opportunities, aren't we?" she wrote several years ago. "Isn't it exciting? Little opportunities, big opportunities. All of us. How can we make it better? How can we make it best? For him. For her. For us. The pursuit of perfection. We may not get there, but we can try. That's vitality. That's the pursuit of life itself. Isn't it?"

With Nick Nolte in Grace Quigley, *1985.* (PHOTOFEST)

Kate with Henry and Jane Fonda. (PHOTOFEST)

Sources

Articles

Christopher Anderson, "In Her Words," *People*, October 11, 1976.

Kenneth Baker, "What's Ahead for Hepburn?" *Photoplay*, July 1934.

Joan Barthel, "Kate at 70," *McCalls*, February 1979.

Kirtley Baskette, "Is Hepburn Killing Her Own Career?" *Photoplay*, September 1935; "What Happened to Hepburn?" *Photoplay*, December 1940.

Carol Craig, "This Is Hepburn," *Movie Classic*, February 1936.

George Cukor, "Forever Katie," *Photoplay*, February 1948.

Jane Ellis, "At Home with Kate," *House Beautiful*, February 1991.

William F. French, "Why Katharine Hepburn Is Different," *Motion Picture Magazine*, February 1936.

Sara Hamilton, "Well, Well, So This Is Hepburn!" *Photoplay*, August 1933.

Caryn James, "Katharine Hepburn, Well Cast in the Drama of Her Life," *The New York Times*, September 1, 1991.

Oliver O. Jensen, "The Hepburns," *Life*, January 22, 1940.

Jocelyn McClurg, "Kate on Kate," *The Saturday Evening Post*, February 1992.

Tom Mathews, "Kate," *Newsweek*, August 31, 1987.

Henry F. Pringle, "A Mind of Her Own," *Collier's,* October 28, 1933.

Bogart Rogers, "The Chap Who Will Never Be Mr. Hepburn," *Photoplay*, March 1935.

Gregory Speck, "Katharine Hepburn," *Interview*, September 1985.

Lupton A. Wilkinson and J. Bryan III, "The Hepburn Story," *The Saturday Evening Post*, November 29, 1941; December 6, 1941; December 13, 1941; December 27, 1941.

Television interview with George Cukor and Katharine Hepburn, June 1969.

Books

Christopher Anderson, *Young Kate*, Henry Holt and Company, 1988.

Gary Carey, *Katharine Hepburn: A Hollywood Yankee*, St. Martin's Press, 1983.

Anne Edwards, *A Remarkable Woman*, William Morrow and Company, 1985.

Katharine Hepburn, *The Making of the African Queen*, Alfred A. Knopf, 1987.

————. *Me, Stories of My Life*, Alfred A. Knopf, 1991.

Charles Higham, *Kate: The Life of Katharine Hepburn*, W. W. Norton & Co., Inc., 1975.

Garson Kanin, *Tracy and Hepburn*, The Viking Press, 1970.

Lauren Tarshis is a writer and editor.
She lives in Connecticut.